THE NIBELUNGENLIED
AN INTERPRETATIVE COMMENTARY

NIBELUN

AN INTERPRETATIVE
COMMENTARY

THE
GENLIED

BY D.G. MOWATT &
HUGH SACKER

UNIVERSITY OF TORONTO PRESS

This book was published with the assistance
of a grant from the Publications Fund of the
University of Toronto Press

Printed in Great Britain by
Hazell Watson & Viney Ltd
Aylesbury, Bucks

5908

CONTENTS

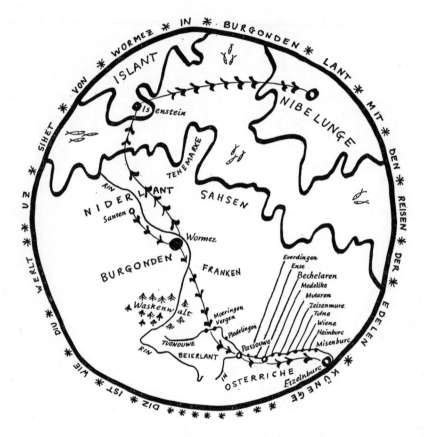

The World of the *Nibelungenlied*: Journeys

The World of the *Nibelungenlied*: Genealogies

AUTHORS' NOTE

The maps on pages vi and vii, which were designed and drawn by Tim and Susan Bahaire, and the diagram on page 28, are intended as visual evocations of important features of the *Nibelungenlied*, and not as comprehensive genealogical or geographical reference works.

INTRODUCTION

✑ INTRODUCTION

The Nibelungenlied is a mediaeval German poem of between nine and ten thousand lines which dates from around 1200. Subdivided into thirty-nine sections or "âventiuren," it is classed as a heroic epic, since it tells in verse of the deeds of kings and the wars of nations in a formulaic and somewhat elevated style. Its end is annihilation for almost all concerned, annihilation unrelieved by any thought of an after-life, Christian or pagan. It is anonymous, virtually nothing being known of the circumstances of its composition. Since its rediscovery in the mid-eighteenth century, the Nibelungenlied has exercised a remarkable fascination, at least in Germany; the literature on it is immense, and it has frequently been compared to the Iliad.

The present Commentary is interpretative, that is, it draws attention to features of the work which, in our view, contribute in an interesting way to its meaning. It is our hope that the Commentary might help to advance modern understanding and enjoyment of a work which has been more praised than appreciated. Our aim has been to stimulate rather than to resolve discussion and reflection, and we make no claim to provide a definitive or authoritative view of the poem. Moreover, we consider that even today, when interpretation of the Nibelungenlied is at last becoming fashionable, much of this interpretation is naïve and elementary; if some of our notes appear to complicate rather than to clarify, it is perhaps because we have tried to be

more detailed and less superficial in our analysis of certain patterns than have most of our predecessors.

This Introduction, with its discussion of scholarly attitudes
towards the Nibelungenlied, aims at a greater degree of generality
than does the Commentary. We are here trying to present the
basis on which the Commentary itself is founded, and to outline
the interpretative framework which is suggested by our more
detailed analysis.

PLOT

The plot centres throughout on the court of Burgundy, which is
presented in the opening âventiure as a model of perfection. Resi-
dent at Worms, it is ruled by King Gunther and his two brothers
Gernot and Giselher, the latter of whom is shown in the course
of the work as a young man in the process of growing up. The
kings have one sister, Kriemhilde, who is the first person to be
introduced, and whose love for a certain Sifrid and revenge of his
murder is one of the principal strands connecting the various
parts of the work. The chief retainer and adviser of the three
kings is Hagen, a man of great experience and determination,
whose relationship to Sifrid during the latter's life is ambivalent
—it is he who in fact murders Sifrid—and who after Sifrid's
death dominates the scene as Kriemhilde's chief antagonist.

The second âventiure is set not at Worms, but at Santen in the
Netherlands, where the young prince Sifrid grows up as an only
child of King Sigemund and Queen Sigelinde. When, having
decided to woo Kriemhilde, Sifrid arrives at Worms in âventiure
3, the action at last begins to get under way, and a new dimension
is introduced into the story. For, as Hagen informs the Burgundians, Sifrid is not just the handsome prince he had appeared at
Worms, but has a magical, superhuman side: he has killed a
dragon and made himself invulnerable by bathing in its blood, and
he has killed the two Nibelung brothers and gained possession of
a fabulous treasure and a magic cloak. As Hagen says, Sifrid is
not a man to cross. And indeed Sifrid, who appears by turns as
brash extrovert, love-sick swain, superhuman strong-man and

over-trusting friend—but never as wise diplomat, never as endowed with insight into human nature—presents quite a problem for the Burgundian court. For the most part following Hagen's advice, the three kings avoid the challenge to fight it out with which Sifrid greets them on arrival, and proceed to entangle him in a situation in which he has to wait for an opportunity to be of service to his hosts. When this opportunity comes, Sifrid seizes it with obvious relish, and wins the war against the Saxons virtually single-handed. Only then, after a year's wait, is he allowed to see Kriemhilde. The initiative throughout this period lies not with Sifrid, who started so confidently, but with outsiders —the Saxons—or with the Burgundians, who proceed now to use Sifrid for an expedition which, without him, would be unthinkable: the winning of the fabulous and redoubtable Brünnhilde as Gunther's wife.

In many ways the antithesis of Kriemhilde, Brünnhilde is an isolated queen, who rules far-off Iceland in her own right, and forces suitors to compete with her in trials of personal strength and to pay for defeat with their lives. Such a challenge, of course, presents little problem (and therefore little attraction?) to the superman in Sifrid, but an immense one to Gunther and the Burgundians. Gunther, whom Sifrid (invisible in his magic cloak) carries under his arm in one trial, and whom Brünnhilde hangs up from a nail on his wedding night, is made to look an utter fool. All concerned behave callously to Brünnhilde, whom they treat as a trophy, as a savage to be used or abused at will, so that it is not surprising that she is never quite content as Gunther's wife and worries continuously about Sifrid. Nevertheless the two couples celebrate a double wedding and live amicably in their separate countries for ten years before there is a further development.

This wedding and subsequent pause mark the conclusion of the first major sequence in the story. In the next sequence, the central act is the murder of Sifrid, which may also be considered the pivot of the whole story, in that everything before leads up to it and everything after follows from it. The slender thread which connects the two sequences—Brünnhilde's discontent—has momentous results, precisely because it touches on every aspect of the Burgundians' situation and their relationship to Sifrid. There follow in quick succession Gunther's invitation to Sifrid and Kriemhilde to visit Worms, the famous quarrel of the two queens, Brünnhilde's humiliation when Kriemhilde flaunts trophies which Sifrid had taken when subduing her for Gunther, and finally Hagen's revenge for this humiliation by the murder of Sifrid. The dramatic quality of the crucial âventiure 14 has been admired by many readers, the overt motivation for both the quarrel and the murder widely deplored as rather thin, the underlying worries of all Burgundians about Sifrid's potentialities hesitantly considered as nebulous but necessary contributory background.

The consequences of the murder are considerable. Sifrid, whose first arrival at Worms sets everything in motion, has been eliminated, and Brünnhilde's role is played out: as a defiant virgin she challenged the world, as a cheated wife she prevented things from stagnating; now, with a barren triumph behind her and the only man who was a match for her dead, she has no function at all, and is gradually forgotten. So, for a time at least, there are once more only native Burgundians on the scene—but they are no longer united. Kriemhilde, who opts, after the murder, for an empty life at Worms rather than return to Santen and find such compensation as she could as Queen of the Netherlands and the mother of Sifrid's son, proceeds to brood for her dead husband. Hagen glories in his deed and provokes her whenever possible. The three kings, led now in this by Giselher, try to appease their consciences and make it up with their sister. Hagen's will dominates for a time, but achieves little: Sifrid's treasure is brought to Worms, stolen from Kriemhilde—but buried in the Rhine. So, after Sifrid's death, there follows a second pause, this time of thirteen years, indicating a protracted stalemate.

The new impetus comes from outside, but its effects show that the long uneasy truce at Worms is only waiting for a spark. This is provided by the decision of King Etzel of Hunland (a vast kingdom centred in Austro-Hungary) to ask Kriemhilde to marry him now that his first wife, Helche, is dead. The decision is taken in council and treated primarily as a matter of state, since the vast peoples, heathen and Christian, over whom Etzel rules need a

mother-figure as well as himself to look to. All Etzel demands personally is that his new wife should also possess some feminine
allure. He seems in general just to want to add Kriemhilde, as the
widow of the famous Sifrid, to the vast collection of illustrious
semi-dependents who surround him, of whom the legendary
Dietrich of Bern is the chief. Not until it is too late does Etzel,
perhaps the least perceptive of a whole series of unperceptive
characters in the work, realize that Kriemhilde does not accept his
offer out of admiration for him or out of any desire to start a new
life, but simply to use him and his legions to assuage her grief in
vengeance—an idea suggested to her, without, it seems, any
realization of what he has done, by Etzel's model ambassador
Rüdeger, who shows here as elsewhere a fine awareness of what
will win him the goodwill of others, but an almost wilful blindness to the harsh underlying realities of the situation.

At last, then, positions are being taken for the final struggle.
In Hunland Kriemhilde has matters all her own way, and slowly
strengthens her hand. She now thinks of nothing but revenge,
and although almost to the end she consciously distinguishes
between her brothers, and especially Giselher, for whom she feels
affection, and Hagen whom she hates, yet she invites all, and
gradually merges her mixed emotions in a single orgy of destruction.

This eventual lack of discrimination about the Burgundians
is in part forced on Kriemhilde as they slowly coalesce once more
into a single entity. Starting at the beginning of the epic as a
unified, complex but static court, they pass through a stage of
inner disunity when Hagen defiantly glories in the murder, while
the three kings are ashamed of it, only to end again united, but
now as a simple and militant army, deliberately courting death in
order not to appear weak or afraid. That the Burgundians assume
this fatal posture is owing to the three kings' consciences, which
lead them to trust their sister blindly, and to Hagen's twofold
nature: he is only the cautious, far-seeing councillor when his
emotions are not personally aroused; underneath there ever lurks
the reckless, self-assertive and unscrupulous old warrior who only
seeks an excuse to murder the trusting superman, and then enjoys
inciting his widow to try to make him regret it.

Given the unperceptiveness of Etzel, the determination of Kriemhilde, and the dangerous ambivalence of the Burgundians, the final catastrophe is inevitable. The grand scale on which this catastrophe is presented is nonetheless impressive; about a third of the total poem is devoted to the Burgundian visit to Etzel, to the "feast" to end all feasts, in which both nations are virtually wiped out. At the very end of the epic, when all grades in the hierarchy of both sides, from the baggage servants through minor and slightly comic individuals like Iring, to Gernot, Rüdeger and Giselher, have been killed, and Hagen and Gunther taken prisoner by Dietrich, then the poet presents the final personal confrontation (after Gunther's death) between the two individuals whom he has built up as personal protagonists, Kriemhilde and Hagen— and has them both ignobly butchered. Thus all the glory of a defiantly accepted war of annihilation has been depicted, and still a personal and pathetic note struck at the end. On this note the poem finishes. All the magnificence, all the manoeuvring, all the defiance has come to this: the killing of Hagen, a prisoner, by Kriemhilde, and the killing of Kriemhilde by a mere retainer, Hildebrant. So much for glory.

INTERPRETATION

The Nibelungenlied is an intriguing story, and one difficult to pin down as to its essential nature. Although several attempts have been made in the last half-century to represent it as a sort of novel about Kriemhilde,[1] this is patently unsatisfactory: she hardly appears at all in the first third of the poem, and even if her will for revenge counts for a lot in the last third, the attention centres on the Burgundians at bay. Indeed, just as much as Kriemhilde's story, it could be considered Hagen's, for, displaced from his central advisory position for a time by Sifrid, Hagen later does away with the usurper, and then leads the Burgundians to glory and death. But if the Nibelungenlied is anyone's story, it is surely

[1] The most recent such attempt, and the fullest, is by Werner Schröder, "Die Tragödie Kriemhilts im Nibelungenlied," Zeitschrift für deutsches Altertum, Vol. XC (1960–61).

the Burgundians' as a whole—the story of their involvement with Sifrid, of Gunther's misplaced marital ambitions, of the consequences for them all of Sifrid's murder; the story of the relationship between Hagen and Sifrid, Hagen and the three kings, all of them and Kriemhilde; the story of the Burgundian encounters with other peoples and finally with the Huns, whom they use for their own destruction.

The minimal descriptive framework might perhaps be that the work shows how a society—the Burgundian court—which begins as unified, static and inflated, becomes fragmented by the effort to absorb alien elements, and only manages to reunite in the simplicity of self-destruction. But to understand this process, one has to give full weight to the alien elements, to the elemental values which link Sifrid with Brünnhilde and Nibelungland, and one has to realize how sharply these contrast with the values of the Burgundians. One also has to accept that Kriemhilde remains throughout a Burgundian, choosing to stay with her own people even when they have killed her husband, working in a sense together with Hagen in the last third of the tale for the annihilation of all. What the *Nibelungenlied* presents is two contrasting ideals —of social control and of instinctual action—hankering for one another; and it shows with what disastrous effects for both they can combine.

Not that this disaster appears internally inevitable from the beginning, in spite of the narrator's frequent references to the end that does in fact come about; the pauses, the human trivialities, the interventions from outside counteract the impression of any single-minded master plan. Several times the story nearly peters out, although always there is a lingering dissatisfaction, an unresolved complication, which either leads to or is receptive of further development. One of the attractions of the *Nibelungenlied* is the way in which the plot thickens and then thins out again —and nevertheless leads to total resolution at the end. Disaster on the scale which is finally achieved is explicable from the nature of the initial encounter, but there is nothing inexorable about the way it is worked out—chance and triviality are given their due.

The unravelling of the plot is narrated impersonally, with detachment, in repetitive phrases, expansively, and with a commentary which lacks all except the most elementary discrimination. Were the story simple and rational, the banality of it all would be extreme. As it is, there is conveyed a feeling that no master-mind was responsible, that this is how things happened—and it is up to the audience to make sense of it or not. According to the narrator, all his tale shows is that happiness always ends in sorrow—an unpretentious cliché which is certainly more appropriate to the story than some that modern critics have supplied, but which remains so detached as to be totally unintrusive. So too, when Hagen murders Sifrid, his treachery is deplored by the narrator, but no attempt is made to explain to the audience how we should reconcile our moral disapproval with the admiration we are made to feel (even to some extent at the time) for his reckless courage and bravado. Such a narrator cannot be regarded as offering an adequate interpretation of the events he records; rather, we are left to treat his comments lightly and supply quite different ones of our own.

The off-hand, repetitive phrases in which the story is told have a similar effect. Deriving almost certainly from a tradition of spontaneous oral poetry, in which the story-teller makes up a more-or-less different version of a traditional tale each time he tells it and is able to keep going only by repetitiveness of phrase and metre (see below, p. 19 ff.), this style too conveys the impression, not of a high-powered intelligence generating at each successive moment the uniquely appropriate phrase for the situation —the ideal of most modern poetry—but of an entertainer who is himself impressed by these stories of long ago and yet keeps his distance, allowing them a good deal of latitude, since he himself only half knows what matters and what does not.

There are, indeed, many signs in the work of a rather threadbare, minimal competence. The poem rambles on repetitiously, lines and stanzas are filled out with padding, new starts occur for no apparent reason, characters are introduced two or three times over, unmistakable changes in style or metre appear to serve no purpose, internal inconsistencies are not uncommon, the sequence of events is often muddled, the passage of time operates in some respects but not in others, the forms *du* and *ir* are sometimes interchanged at random, the pairs or groups in which the characters confer or dispute are broken up and reformed more in the fashion of dreams than of reality, characters behave now in one way, now in a seemingly incompatible way, without anyone remarking on the change—there is simply no attempt to make everything fit. This frequent unconcern with the logic of detail is, however, not all that disturbing. Partly it is counteracted by our perception of a deliberate and largely successful effort on the part of the author (or authors) to impose some sort of order on recalcitrant material, but more essentially, in our view, by the fact that it is on this basis of casual disorder that many of the most successful effects of the work are founded.

Let us first of all indicate some results of conscious control on the part of the poet, all elementary, but nonetheless satisfying. There is, for instance, the general balance of the work: the fact that it divides into two approximately equal halves before and after Etzel's appearance on the scene—or again, into three more or less equal parts, dividing first after Sifrid's murder and then before Kriemhilde invites her kinsmen to Hunland. There is the Bechelaren interlude, where an idyllic pause is strategically placed just before the grim finality of the last battles. There is the way in which Volker—a Burgundian minstrel who plays no part in the first two thirds of the story, but who emerges as Hagen's most unconditional support in the last third—is yet mentioned a few times early on to prepare us for his later importance. So too, if the Saxon war is a muddle, there is the carefully controlled progression of the battles at Etzel's court.

Again, if idealising adjectives are in general rather indiscriminately applied to everyone, nevertheless Sifrid is more often described as "strong" than anyone else, and Hagen alone frequently appears as "grim." The anticipations of disaster which are scattered throughout the epic and which are apparently used simply to fill out certain stanzas, nevertheless seem to be grouped in a more or less sensible manner; for instance, in the very first âventiure we find three separate ones (2,4; 6,4; 19,4), of which each anticipates a different event in the future and which together span the whole work, while in the following three âventiuren there are hardly any at all. Also, if the murder of the Danube ferryman is rather puzzling, and Hagen's feat of rowing the whole army of

10,000 across the river single-handed a bit improbable, yet it is clear that the crossing as a whole is a well utilized symbol: before it the Burgundians still hope for a way back, after it they increasingly brace themselves to face certain death. Lastly, if it is an insoluble problem just why the name Nibelungs, which in the first two-thirds of the poem is reserved for the inhabitants of the land where Sifrid's treasure came from, from the time of the Danube crossing is frequently applied to the Burgundians, there is something rather touching in the way the text apparently tries to ease the transition for us by mentioning at this very point that some of Sifrid's original Nibelungs accompany the Burgundians on their last journey (see note to stanza 1526). All of these features, and many more, bear witness to a conscious control applied to recalcitrant material by some ordering mind—and depend for their appeal precisely on their only partial effectiveness. A systematically and efficiently controlled work would make a very different impression.

There are two rather more general features which, like those just listed, are commonly admired today, and which were probably also largely intended by the author or authors. One is the dramatic tension and density of a number of scenes, such as those presenting the first arrival of Sifrid at Worms, the quarrel between the two queens, or the confrontation of Hagen and Kriemhilde shortly after the Burgundians arrive at Etzel's court. The effect of such scenes depends partly on the tensely charged dialogue, but perhaps even more on their general role in the work; in them conflicts which are latent suddenly explode, exposing dramatically before our eyes hidden tensions more intense than we knew, and by the explosion providing further impetus for the future. Many of these scenes were first composed centuries earlier for the short lays that were the forerunners of our *Nibelungenlied*, but they were retained, adapted and even initiated by whoever composed this latter, and it is difficult to believe that they have not always been appreciated.

Also generally admired, if sometimes reluctantly, with some degree of bafflement, is the overall structure of the plot: the way the courtship of Sifrid leads over to his murder and the widowhood of Kriemhilde, and this in turn to her second marriage and revenge on her kinsmen. There can be little doubt that this structure was more or less consciously contrived, and that, whatever the problems it throws up, its contriving was a remarkable achievement. Without it, the work would fail on an elementary level and lose much of its appeal, at least for the general reader.

Most of what has been said so far is generally agreed: the *Nibelungenlied* appears to many as an intriguing combination of incompetence and contrivance.[2] But does this mixture, together with the plot, account for the remarkable hold it exercises on its readers? Has enough now been said about the work itself, and do we now need to turn to its sources and to the background of mediaeval culture in order to appreciate it further? Certainly these extraneous factors partially account for the rather patronizing admiration of the *Nibelungenlied* shown by some readers, but we suggest that much of its hold on the imagination derives from an interplay of elements which was probably not consciously intended by the mediaeval author (or authors) and which has not to any appreciable extent been analyzed by modern critics. This interplay depends for its success on the relationships between the consciously controlled overall structure and the material itself, the individual elements which appear to some extent out of control. These two levels of phenomena, conscious design and seemingly random detail, are linked together in elusive and unpredictable, but nonetheless extremely revealing and significant ways.

It is, for instance, only from this point of view that the various characters become really interesting. Consider Kriemhilde. The work reveals a consciousness that as a girl she was demure, as a wife proud, when newly widowed grief-stricken, at the end a she-devil murdering tens of thousands for a personal vendetta. But no comment is passed on the relationship of these stages to one another. Thus while some modern readers have maintained that the stages are not integrally connected—Kriemhilde just playing the particular role required by each situation in turn—others believe equally firmly that they constitute the main point of the

[2] Friedrich Panzer's book, *Das Nibelungenlied: Entstehung und Gestalt* (Stuttgart, 1955), contains further detailed information on many aspects of the epic mentioned here, but offers no adequate interpretation.

poem and present a straightforward characterological sequence.[3] Each of these verdicts can be supported by reference to the mediaeval background, to other works in which the development of the main characters is minimal or maximal, but neither of them is adequate to the situation. The simple fact is surely that this sort of presentation provides a challenge, a provocation to wonder about human nature as portrayed in this poem. Progress cannot be made by denying the problem, but only by abstracting this and other patterns until common features become apparent.

The results, if not simple, can be illuminating. For instance, if Kriemhilde appears initially as shy and retiring, later as demonic-ally possessed, she is nowhere shown as enjoying easy, yet actively reciprocal relationships with others, nowhere as behaving in a positively creative and outgoing manner. And if the likelihood of such behaviour is regarded as small in the largely male world that is portrayed, yet it will be seen that Kriemhilde reacts to the limitations imposed on women in a man's world differently from any other character. When told by her mother that she can only be fulfilled by a man's love, she says in that case she will remain beautiful as she is. Brought up by her brothers in unusual seclu-sion, she goes out of her way to encourage the eldest of them to domineer over her, at least nominally, and to dispose of her as he likes (cf. 356,1–2; 613,1–4). Sought out by and married to the only truly outgoing and spontaneous man in the poem, who is also (not surprisingly) the strongest individual, as well as some-what brash, she at once lays claim on his behalf to a share in her brothers' possessions, or, failing that, to their chief retainer, Hagen, and later provokes the fatal quarrel with Brünnhilde by the superbly ingenuous remark that all the Burgundian lands should be Sifrid's. (Of course, by the simple standards to which Sifrid tends to revert and which she is now invoking as she looks at him in all his manly splendour, this is true; for if the disposal of Bur-gundy, and of herself, had been settled by recourse to arms, as Sifrid first suggested, he would doubtless have taken the lot.) Thus Kriemhilde may be considered to show signs even in the first third of the *Nibelungenlied* of both a preoccupation with domination

[3] This problem is discussed by A. T. Hatto in his translation of the *Nibe-lungenlied* (London, 1965), pp. 312–16.

and power, and a (typically Burgundian) inability to act openly
and directly.

Under these circumstances, Sifrid may well represent Kriemhilde's one chance of getting away from herself, of becoming part
of a simpler and more straightforward nature. Once he is married,
however, Sifrid shows the same casual disregard for her personality and needs that he shows for those of all others—a characteristic largely responsible for his death—and gives her tokens of his
manly exploits without apparently bothering to explain much
about them or to think what she might use them for. And in
fact, when she uses them as support in her quarrel with Brünnhilde (over which of their husbands is pre-eminent—no trivial
issue for either of them), all Sifrid does is to treat it as silly
women's talk and give her a thrashing.

On this level there is not all that much difference between
Kriemhilde's relationship with Sifrid and that of the other Burgundians. She, like them, is preoccupied with the protocol of
power and is not naturally outgoing. For her, as for them, Sifrid
appears to represent a liberation, a new range of activity which
only he can offer. But for her, as for them, he brings with him an
insouciance which is irreconcilable with their deepest worries.
And so it is not surprising that it is in the name of Burgundian
kinship that Kriemhilde, remembering even as she does so that
there could be reasons for not trusting any of her relatives, betrays
Sifrid to Hagen (see note to 893,4). Moreover, she opens the scene
by expressing her pleasure that she has a husband so able to help
her kinsmen, and then, after revealing that the noble man
thrashed her for her trouble-making, proceeds to confess that her
one worry for him is that his *übermuot* might lead him into
danger—although it is only through her intervention at this precise moment that this danger could prove real. It is largely because
of the correlation on some unconscious but perfectly convincing
level between the precise phrasing of such a scene and the gener-
alities of the overall structure of the triangle Burgundians-
Kriemhilde-Sifrid that, in our opinion, the *Nibelungenlied* makes
the deep appeal it does make.

The particular aspect considered here can be extended (with
appropriate modification and development) in every direction.

The treasure, something which only a Sifrid can acquire but in which a Sifrid has no interest, becomes in the hands of the Burgundians an inert lump which fascinates Hagen and Kriemhilde, even though neither of them understands its nature (cf. notes to 1134,1–3 and 1739,3). Also, once it has been seen how Kriemhilde and Hagen join to destroy Sifrid, it can be better understood that they join to destroy their society and themselves in his name. Certainly they fight, but they are fighting from a common standpoint to a common goal—and it is only on this level that Kriemhilde's refusal to leave Burgundy after the murder and Hagen's subsequent unremitting provocation of her can be understood.

To develop such points, and to suggest in detail how particular phrases and scenes are linked with remarkable precision to the overall structure is not the task of this Introduction, but of the notes to individual passages which follow in the Commentary. The object here is to provide a background for these notes by indicating in general terms what kind of work the *Nibelungenlied* is. In it disregard for logic and consistency at a commonsense level is more marked than in most other works, even of its own time. This disregard is tempered by a degree of rational control which provides some sort of commonsense framework, but which is not itself adequate to explain the appeal of the poem. This appeal is, however, explicable to a large extent in terms of the correlation between apparently random detail and overall structure at a fairly high degree of abstraction—a correlation which very probably exists in all great works of art, but which, in the case of the *Nibelungenlied*, is intimately related to the apparent carelessness of composition.

METRE

The *Nibelungenlied* is composed of short stanzas, each consisting of four long lines with a break or caesura in the middle. The long lines rhyme in pairs (aabb) and the end of each stanza is marked by the distinctive metre of the last half-line. The stanzaic form distinguishes the *Nibelungenlied* (and *Kudrun*) from almost all

German mediaeval narrative verse, the normal metre of which is the short rhyming couplet, and links it up with the lyric, which was also composed in stanzas. In particular, some of the extant lyrics of the *Kürenberger* (probably an Austrian poet of around 1160) show a virtually identical form to the *Nibelungenlied*. It is, however, uncertain just what conclusions should be drawn from this—except that the poet (or poets) of the *Nibelungenlied* shunned the normal metrical tradition of the literary epic and perhaps looked to local lyrical practice in inventing a form of his (or their) own.

Normally, each half-line has three full stresses, and the caesura shows an (unrhymed) feminine ending, while the long line ends with a masculine rhyme. Stressed syllables tend to be separated from one another by a single unstressed syllable, but considerable freedom is allowed. Stanza 82, for example, can be scanned quite regularly:

Dém sint kúnt diu ríche   und óuch diu vrémden lánt.
sint ím die hérren künde,   daz túot er úns bekánt.
der künec bát in bríngen   únd die sínen mán.
man sách in hérlìche   mit récken hín ze hóve gán.

In this example, the last half-line of the stanza is marked by having four full stresses. Frequently, however, it only has three, but in that case the second stress always falls on a grammatically long syllable, and between the second and third full stresses there occur two syllables, of which the first is capable of bearing a secondary stress:

80,4   dáz was Gúnthère léit
83,4   der réhten wárheìte jéhen
85,4   si wáeren hóhè gemúot

Thus, one way or the other, the end of the stanza is always metrically defined.

Slight variants on this metre occur. In particular, a number of stanzas are found with caesura rhyme (e.g. stanza 1), and there are some in which the second halves of the opening pair of long lines have only two full stresses each and a feminine ending (e.g. stanza 1715). Historians regard the former as a late variation on the metre, and the latter as an early variation. Neither type of variation is so marked as to disturb the reader very much—and both seem to be employed with little concern for effect.

The rhymes are of the type usually described as "full" or "pure": the last stressed vowel and all subsequent letters are identical. This is the normal type of rhyme found in the better verse of the day. "Impure" rhyme (or "assonance"), in which some of the letters specified are not identical, occurs occasionally; it is most common, and indeed almost a metrical motif, when rhyming Hagene (e.g. 83,1–2).

The syntax usually fits neatly into the metrical unit: a syntactic group ending with each half-line, a clause running on to the end of the line, a new topic often beginning with a new stanza. Thus, small pauses usually occur at the end of each half-line, larger ones at the end of the long line, and still more marked ones at the end of the stanza. The rhythmic effect produced suggests more a static rocking to and fro than a fast progression, an effect which would be unsuitable for narrative verse, were it not modified by gently varying leads from one unit to the next (e.g. stanzas 81–83).

Gentle variation is indeed a key factor in the metre, from whatever aspect this is regarded. One can abstract a norm, but most stanzas and most lines are in fact variants on it. To a limited extent the variants are used to support the sense (as, for instance, when *hérlìche* bears two adjacent stresses in 82,4). It is, however, doubtful whether the metre would bear too close an examination from this point of view. In general the repetitiousness and the variations just carry the reader along pleasantly, and only here and there are the expressive possibilities exploited to the full. The parallel with the other aspects of the artistry of the work is obvious (see above, pp. 9–12).

GENESIS

Having tried to give some idea of what the Nibelungenlied is like, one arrives at the question: how did it come to be like this? This is a problem to which a vast amount of research has been devoted, but about which very little has been discovered.

One difficulty is that, as already stated, the Nibelungenlied is unique: there is only one at all similar poem deriving from roughly the same place and time, Kudrun, and it is largely dependent for its inspiration on the Nibelungenlied. Both poems are anonymous, and we do not know with any certainty what sort of persons composed them, nor for what kind of audience. But whereas Kudrun exists only in one early sixteenth-century manuscript, the Nibelungenlied was very successful: thirty-four manuscripts or fragments of it are extant, and that is more than exist of most works of Middle High German literature. From these manuscripts, from points in the text and from references to the Nibelungenlied in other works, we can infer with reasonable certainty that it was composed within a few years of 1200, probably just after the turn of the century, and most likely in Austria. But little else about its origins is certain.

In these circumstances one obvious course is to turn to similar modern literature, and to investigate under what circumstances it is composed.[4] Such comparison will not prove anything about the Nibelungenlied, but it may offer useful guidance. The most similar literature of this type to have been investigated at all thoroughly is the popular epic of the Serbo-Croats. This epic was made known to Nibelungenlied scholars fifty years ago through the pioneer work of Matija Murko, and has since been more fully recorded and described by Milman Parry and A. B. Lord.[5] Parry and Lord describe this poetry as "oral-formulaic," since its tradition is entirely oral, and its style is characterized by the use of repetitive formulae. The story-tellers who purvey it do not learn their stories by heart, and never repeat

[4] Cf. Roman Jakobson in Serbocroatian Heroic Songs, edited by A. B. Lord, Vol. I (Cambridge, Mass., 1954), p. xi: "The modern science of language has come to realise that the most efficient way to obtain a thorough understanding of the linguistic events of the past is to study closely the linguistic processes which we ourselves witness. Descriptive study in general, and the description of the contemporary status in particular, is a necessary first step towards a deeper and more comprehensive historical approach."

[5] See the Select Bibliography, p. 33, for a number of works in this field, of which A. B. Lord's The Singer of Tales (Cambridge, Mass., 1960) provides the most general introduction.

them twice in the same way; they have instead a stock of themes which they modulate each time, as inspiration and circumstances require. Their poems are nowhere near as long as the *Nibelungenlied*, but occasionally, if asked to dictate a poem to a scribe and freed from the necessity of confining their whole tale within a single session, they produce better and longer versions than usual. Parry and Lord believe that the Homeric poems derived from such a tradition and were perhaps thus dictated—and Lord would favour a similar theory for *Beowulf* and the *Nibelungenlied*.

The general style of the *Nibelungenlied* certainly accords with Lord's specifications—which include repetitive formulae (together with repetitive situations, such as are also found in the *Nibelungenlied*), paratactic syntax, and a certain inconsequentiality. Moreover, there is a great deal of evidence that the themes of the *Nibelungenlied*, especially those of Sifrid's supernatural youth, his murder, and the annihilation of the Burgundians, were spread throughout northern Europe for almost a thousand years in short lays narrated, now in one form, now in another, by oral poets. (No other probable explanation can account for the following facts: that the destruction of the Burgundians by the Huns under Attila must date from historical events of the fifth century A.D.; that the Icelandic *Edda*, written down in the thirteenth century, but dating in part from the ninth, contain slightly differing versions of all three themes; that a thirteenth-century Norwegian compilation called the *Thidrekssaga* contains, among other stories relating more or less closely to Dietrich of Bern, some episodes very close to those of the *Nibelungenlied*; that as late as 1500 or so a mediaeval story was put together about *Hürnen Seyfrid*; and that, whereas there do exist a number of similar and related lays and legends and some references to them in other literature and chronicles, there was no famous and widely read written source from which all these could have derived.)

So the themes of the *Nibelungenlied* must have been known in twelfth-century Austria from oral tradition. But in precisely what form were these themes known, and how had they changed through the centuries? These questions, which have been much investigated, are perhaps asked in vain. For whereas Andreas Heusler, who wrote the most famous monograph on the subject,

Nibelungensage und Nibelungenlied, maintained that each stage in the development must be the creation of a single great poet and would establish the form of the saga until another great poet altered it, Parry and Lord have discovered that oral poets vary their themes all the time—and doubt whether these variations can ever be tracked down. And since *Nibelungenlied* scholars have not managed to achieve unanimity on this subject, perhaps Parry and Lord are right.

In any case, from the present point of view—that of understanding not exactly what existed before the *Nibelungenlied* but in what sort of situation the *Nibelungenlied* such as we know it came to be composed—the combination of information from Parry and Lord about oral poetry among the Serbo-Croats and from mediaevalists about the nature of the *Nibelungenlied* and the history of its themes does suggest that its background was an oral-formulaic tradition of short ballads and possibly short epics on the various themes involved, and that these poems may very well have been composed more or less freely at every performance. What would be rash would be to assume that our *Nibelungenlied* was also composed by such an oral poet. Like the Homeric poems, the *Nibelungenlied* is in a different class from the common run of oral poetry from which it probably derives. Whether such uniquely long and impressive poems are the product of an oral poet's dictating, or of a literary poet's adapting the idiom of oral poetry, or of any possible combination of or variation on these alternatives, we do not know. All we can say is that this is the probable literary background, and that they transcend it. Even the belief that such works can only be the product of a single great poet—barely questioned in the last fifty years—need not be maintained dogmatically on present evidence.

What about the social and ideological background? The social status of both poet and audience has been discussed at considerable length, though perhaps too much from the literary historian's and too little from the sociologist's viewpoint. Earlier scholars mostly thought that the poet was a travelling minstrel, more recent ones that he was a (landless) knight or a cleric. The audience was earlier felt to have been (at least to some extent) the common people, nowadays it is believed that it was probably the more exalted courts of Austria. The somewhat excessive attention paid in the poem to the Bishop of Passau is frequently, and not unreasonably, held to suggest that Wolfger von Erla, Bishop of Passau from 1191 to 1204 and a considerable patron of literature, may also have been the person for whom our *Nibelungenlied* was composed. In general, however, the sociological implications of the poem bear further investigation. It is probable that there is not simply an ideological, but also a sociological gulf between the literary Arthurian epics of the day, with all their Christian and chivalrous idealism, and the detached and rather disillusioned objectivity of the *Nibelungenlied*. Students interested in such problems might proceed in two directions: by investigating twentieth-century societies in which diverse poetic traditions are found, and by further analysing the structure of Austrian society around 1200. Only then could the various possibilities be distinguished from one another and further refined.

Another question which can be and has been asked is where and how the *Nibelungenlied* connects up with the *Geistesgeschichte* of mediaeval Germany. What is its relationship to the religious and intellectual history of the time? The temptation here is to take the elements which have gone into the making of the whole and discuss their origins rather than the uses to which they are put. Since the old lays were probably pagan in origin and heroic in spirit, whereas the court scenes clearly derived from contemporary court life which was undoubtedly Christian, according to one view the *Nibelungenlied* represents an attempt around 1200 to unite the pagan heroic tradition with the softer humanity of certain forms of Christianity. And possibly in the genesis of the poem some such process may have played a part.

But the *Nibelungenlied* has absorbed its component parts. In the finished work the fighting heroism and the diplomatic pretension are both universally human: they are present in all societies and familiar to all men. The Christianity is identical in its superficiality with that of many people today. What in the last analysis characterizes the ethos of the poem is not these elements, but the sophisticated detachment and admiring disillusion which the narrator maintains throughout, and which the story finally justifies: life has its moments, and its pattern, but there is little left in the end. This attitude, as has already been said, may better be explained by reference to sociological grouping than to the history of the times. It is a common characteristic of the intelligent underdog.

As for the age in which the epic was written, it was a transitional age, in which for a brief generation or two a humane culture suddenly flourished in the Middle Ages. The reign of Frederick Barbarossa (1152–90) had given a romantic boost to German chivalry, which seemed to be spreading into France and Italy—and even to Palestine. The courts flourished with a lighter touch than ever before, and were not yet wholly cut off from the people. The gloomy preaching of earlier and later centuries was temporarily subordinated to worldly chronicles, romances and the new vogue for French love-songs. The Augustinian emphasis on predestination and the sacraments was yielding to a Thomist conception of all as erring children of the Father. It was a worldly age, and an expansive one—but short-lived, for when Barbarossa's gifted son Henry VI died young in 1197, the country drifted into civil war, and the civilization of chivalry entered its long period of decay (during which the new cultures of the later Middle Ages, the great courts and the towns, gradually developed). A precise connection between an age and a literary work cannot be expected, but that an age of this type should see submerged literary themes rise to the surface and achieve new greatness is not perhaps surprising.

SCHOLARSHIP

As has been indicated, the *Nibelungenlied* contains many weaknesses and inconsistencies, and it survives in nearly three dozen divergent manuscripts. But it is strangely impressive.

Faced with these facts, scholars can either collate all the evidence and try to reconstruct better "original" versions, or they can study any one particularly impressive manuscript and try to see what sort of a work it is. Or, of course, they can combine these two approaches—though that usually leads to muddle and compromise.

The history of *Nibelungenlied* scholarship shows that, for the whole of the nineteenth and part of the twentieth century, scholars concentrated on reconstruction. The manuscripts were sorted by Karl Lachmann in the early nineteenth century into three groups, each group being named after a particular manuscript A, B or C. Some fifty years later, Karl Bartsch brought evidence to suggest that A was only an abbreviated version of B, and that therefore there were only two main groups, representing a version close to the original (B), and an expanded version (C). Bartsch's editions of B are still the standard ones used, and his dictionary of the *Nibelungenlied* is the most valuable aid to Nibelungenlied scholarship produced to date. In 1900 Wilhelm Braune published a brilliant study of the relationships between the manuscripts, *Die Handschriftenverhältnisse des Nibelungenliedes*, which is probably the best work of its kind on mediaeval German. He too gave priority to manuscript B. Recently, however, it has been argued in detail by Helmut Brackert (*Beiträge zur Handschriftenkritik des Nibelungenliedes*) that Braune's work was based on false assumptions and biased by unproven premises; Brackert suggests that the manuscript tradition of the *Nibelungenlied* is so interwoven that any attempt to reconstruct an oldest version must necessarily fail. Possibly, then, we should now start analysing the individual extant manuscripts one by one as interrelated linguistic and literary texts, without bothering too much about which came first, and without attempting to improve on them at all.[6]

Karl Lachmann also produced a classic monograph on the origins of the story, *Über die ursprüngliche Gestalt des Gedichtes von der Nibelungen Noth*. Influenced by similar attitudes to Homer, he believed the *Nibelungenlied* to consist of short lays strung together with connecting material—and in his 1841 edition of manuscript C he distinguished twenty such supposedly original lays by different type. The mid-nineteenth century saw a bitter battle fought over this *Liedertheorie*, which was eventually abandoned. But later nineteenth-century scholars who believed the *Nibelungenlied* to be a single unified work still did not rate it very

[6] For a defence of Braune's work against Brackert, see Werner Schröder's characteristically shrewd, detailed, and deeply conservative review in *Anzeiger für deutsches Altertum*, Vol. LXXVII (1966).

highly, and sought to distinguish older strata within it. So, a century after Lachmann, there appeared a second classic mono-graph, *Nibelungensage und Nibelungenlied*, by Andreas Heusler, who sketched out a development from two original short lays to a twelfth-century lay and a short epic ("die ältere Not", covering the second half of the final work)—and then to the extant version, which he only really admired in so far as it retained the old heroic virtues.

Heusler's theory appears today as the neatest possible recon-struction of the sources, but unfortunately not therefore particu-larly compelling. The work of Parry and Lord already mentioned makes it doubtful whether the development of themes over several centuries can be reconstructed even in outline, and so we are left with the extant versions: the Eddic lays, the *Thidrekssaga*, the *Hürnen Seyfrid*—and the manuscript versions of our *Nibelun-genlied*.

The last fifty years have seen a gradual shift of attention from reconstruction to interpretation. Interpreters have, however, maintained that a scholarly approach is only possible from the mediaeval background, and have failed to realize that such illum-ination as has been attained has originated almost without excep-tion in direct observation of the structure of the work itself, and has only subsequently been linked up with theories about its background.

Until the last few years, the chief insistence has been that the sources must be taken into account whenever the finished work is discussed, and this view is still widely held. Indeed, from Körner and Tonnelat to Nagel and Hatto we find an ad hoc compromise between source analysis and critical appreciation: common sense reveals merits and faults in the work; both are historically condi-tioned, and beyond this we cannot go.

It is the merit of Gottfried Weber (*Das Nibelungenlied. Problem und Idee*, 1963) and his assistant Werner Hoffmann that they have broken categorically with this compromise. They see clearly that source investigation is perfectly justified, but that it must be separated sharply from critical analysis. The function of an ele-ment in the finished work may be similar to its function in the source, but it may be, and more probably is, quite dissimilar—and to determine its function in the finished work we can only study this latter. There is no bridge between the two, however much we might wish for one. But unfortunately, Weber—whose critical insights into the *Nibelungenlied* are of a higher calibre than those of any earlier scholar—insists in the last resort on subordinating them to generalizations about the spirit of the age, which are not only extremely doubtful but also so abstract as to be virtually meaningless.[7]

This obsession with *Geistesgeschichte* dates, of course, from the generation of German scholars between the wars of 1914–18 and 1939–45, and may be expected to die out with this generation. Yet it is clear that scholars will continue to seek historical support of one kind or another for their opinions: they feel too exposed without it. We doubt whether such support is usually worth having. If one is to have any hope of doing justice to a great work of imaginative literature, one must approach it with an open awareness and a fullness of experience that is not confined to a carefully acquired yet extremely limited knowledge of a remote historical period, but that includes instead everything one has met with, read about or can conceive. To seek to approach a literary work as its contemporary audience did is both a futile goal—for even the most learned scholar knows next to nothing about that audience—and an undesirable one, for contemporary audiences seldom appreciate and almost never understand great works produced in their midst. (That the *Nibelungenlied* was little understood at the time is suggested by its continuation, known as *Die Klage*, which follows it in virtually all manuscripts. This sentimentalizing banality, which most modern scholars reject as worthless, appears to have been accepted by the mediaeval audience as an essential continuation of the *Nibelungenlied*.)

The modern reader who approaches the *Nibelungenlied* in the way suggested here will notice, for example, that the Christianity in it is as superficial as often in society today, that Hagen's play with his sword on his encounter with Kriemhilde at Etzel's court resembles the rituals of gunmen in western films, that the empty protestations of Gunther are familiar to him from politi-

---

[7] See further the review of Weber's book by D. G. Mowatt in *German Quarterly*, Vol. XXXVIII (1965), pp. 68–70.

cians on television. The mediaevalist may also note parallels in other mediaeval works (we have ourselves suggested a number of these in the Commentary which follows). But if either amateur or expert wants to be more accurate, to check and control and refine his initial perceptions, he must do so by determining precisely how the elements he has noted are used in the work itself. Possibly his first impressions will be wrong, certainly they will need development. This development, however, should not consist primarily in evolving generalizations about the Middle Ages or in searching for further parallels in other mediaeval works, but in analysing what actually occurs in the particular work under study.

In our opinion, there has been a deal of obscurantism in the mediaeval literary scholarship of the past 150 years. Learned men have patronized the literary masterpieces of the Middle Ages and reduced them to historical curios. But these works rise above their age; they arrange historically conditioned elements in patterns of universal validity and can only be adequately appreciated by a critical, not by an historical approach. In this Introduction we have sought to sketch out the general lines of a possible critical approach to one such work, the *Nibelungenlied*. The Commentary which follows provides more detailed notes on some of its particular features.

THE NETWORK OF RELATIONSHIPS

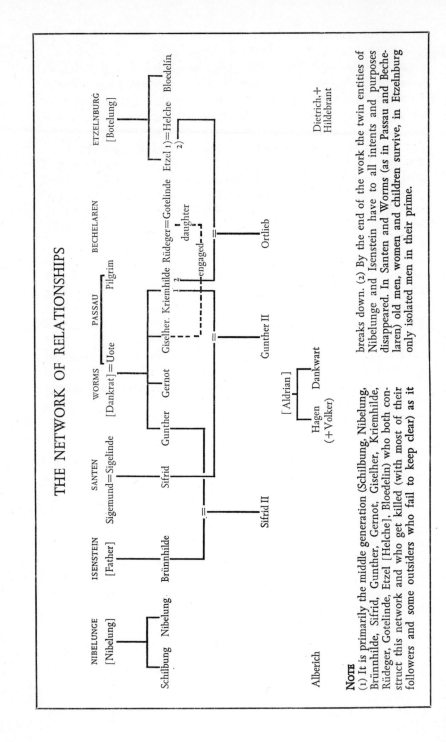

NOTE
(1) It is primarily the middle generation (Schilbung, Nibelung, Brünnhilde, Sifrid, Gunther, Gernot, Giselher, Kriemhilde, Rüdeger, Gotelinde, Etzel [Helche, Bloedelin]) who both construct this network and who get killed (with most of their followers and some outsiders who fail to keep clear) as it breaks down. (2) By the end of the work the twin entities of Nibelunge and Isenstein have to all intents and purposes disappeared. In Santen and Worms (as in Passau and Bechelaren) old men, women and children survive, in Etzelnburg only isolated men in their prime.

⚥ SELECT
BIBLIOGRAPHY

The literature on the *Nibelungenlied* is enormous. Only an initial orientation is attempted here.

A ▪ TEXTS AND TRANSLATIONS

The *Nibelungenlied* is usually read today in an edited version of the manuscripts comprising the B group (see above, p. 24). Karl Bartsch produced both a large critical edition of this version (3 vols., Leipzig, 1870–80), and a smaller annotated one (1st edition, Leipzig, 1866); the last edition revised by Bartsch was the 6th, (Leipzig, 1886). At present, students mostly use Helmut de Boor's revision of this latter (13th edition, Wiesbaden, 1956), but de Boor's notes are more ambitious than Bartsch's, and in our opinion distract from the text. James Boyd's plain text (Oxford, 1948) follows the Bartsch edition. A photographic facsimile of manuscript B has recently been published (*Deutsche Texte in Handschriften*, Vol. I, edited by K. Bischoff, H. M. Heinrichs and W. Schröder, Cologne and Graz, 1962).

Manuscript A was edited by Karl Lachmann (Berlin, 1826; 6th edition, with some additional material by Ulrich Pretzel and Willy Krogmann, Berlin, 1960).

Manuscript C was edited both by Friedrich Zarncke (Leipzig, 1856), and by Adolf Holtzmann (Stuttgart, 1857).

Of the many German translations, those by Hermann Stodte

(Stuttgart, 1939; reprinted 1956) and Helmut de Boor (Bremen, 1959) can both be recommended.
    Of recent English translations, that by D. G. Mowatt (Everyman Library, London and New York, 1962) naturally is closest in spirit to the present Commentary. A. T. Hatto's translation (Penguin Books, London, 1965) is followed by an extensive discussion of many aspects of the work. H. M. Mustard's (in *Mediaeval Epics*, New York, 1963) abbreviates the original on occasion.

B ▪ DICTIONARY

As the third volume of his large critical edition, Karl Bartsch published an indispensable dictionary of the *Nibelungenlied*, which sets out to list all words found in the main manuscripts (*Der Nibelunge Not*, Part II, 2 : *Wörterbuch*, Leipzig, 1880; reprint announced 1967).

C ▪ MONOGRAPHS

The first three monographs listed here contain brilliant statements of approaches to the *Nibelungenlied* which, if no longer entirely valid, were all landmarks of scholarship in their day, and still deserve attention. The remaining studies indicate the uncertain course of *Nibelungenlied* scholarship in the past half-century; a truly classic study from a modern point of view remains to be written.

    1. Karl Lachmann, *Über die ursprüngliche Gestalt des Gedichtes von der Nibelungen Noth* (Berlin, 1816).
    2. Wilhelm Braune, *Die Handschriftenverhältnisse des Nibelungenliedes*, in *Beiträge zur Geschichte der deutschen Sprache und Literatur*, Vol. XXV (1900).
    3. Andreas Heusler, *Nibelungensage und Nibelungenlied* (Dortmund, 1921).
    4. Josef Körner, *Das Nibelungenlied* (Leipzig and Berlin, 1921).
    5. Ernest Tonnelat, *La chanson des Nibelungen* (Paris, 1926).
    6. Nelly Dürrenmatt, *Das Nibelungenlied im Kreis der höfischen Dichtung* (Dissertation, Bern, 1945).

7. Kurt Wais, *Frühe Epik Westeuropas und die Vorgeschichte des Nibelungenliedes* (Tübingen, 1953).

8. Friedrich Panzer, *Das Nibelungenlied: Entstehung und Gestalt* (Stuttgart, 1955).

9. Burghart Wachinger, *Studien zum Nibelungenlied: Vorausdeutungen, Aufbau, Motivierung* (Tübingen, 1960).

10. Helmut Brackert, *Beiträge zur Handschriftenkritik des Nibelungenliedes*, in *Quellen und Forschungen*, Neue Folge Vol. XI (Berlin, 1963).

11. Werner A. Mueller, *The Nibelungenlied Today* (Chapel Hill, 1962).

12. Gottfried Weber, *Das Nibelungenlied: Problem und Idee* (Stuttgart, 1963).

13. Bert Nagel, *Das Nibelungenlied: Stoff, Form, Ethos* (Frankfurt-am-Main, 1965).

D ▪ REFERENCE WORKS

A valuable account in English of *Nibelungenlied* scholarship up to 1939 is given in Mary Thorp, *The Study of the Nibelungenlied* (Oxford, 1940). This can be supplemented and brought up to date by the short handbook that Gottfried Weber and Werner Hoffmann produced for the *Sammlung Metzler: Nibelungenlied* (Stuttgart, 1961). The bibliographical list by Willy Krogmann and Ulrich Pretzel is very handy: *Bibliographie zum Nibelungenlied und zur Klage* (3rd edition, Hamburg, 1960). All books and all articles treating the *Nibelungenlied* are listed year by year in the quarterly bibliographical journal *Germanistik* (Tübingen, 1960 ff.).

The various histories and encyclopaedias of mediaeval German literature can also be consulted with profit. Fairly recent ones of some standing include:

1. Wolfgang Stammler and Karl Langosch (eds.), *Die deutsche Dichtung des Mittelalters. Verfasserlexikon* (Vol. III, 1943, and Vol. V, 1955, contain articles on the *Nibelungenlied* by Friedrich Neumann).

2. Helmut de Boor, *Geschichte der deutschen Literatur*, Vol. II: *Die höfische Literatur* (Munich, 1953).
3. M. O'C. Walshe, *Medieval German Literature* (London, 1962).

E ▪ ARTICLES

Of the many articles published on the *Nibelungenlied* in the last decade or so, only a few can be listed here. They represent various aspects of research, and only the first one listed, by W. J. Schröder, requires special mention. This article has been brushed aside by most subsequent writers, but it seems to us, whatever its faults, to have been the very first study to have shown truly valuable insight into the structure of the *Nibelungenlied*.

1. Walther Johannes Schröder, "Das Nibelungenlied. Versuch einer Deutung," *Beiträge zur Geschichte der deutschen Sprache und Literatur*, Vol. LXXVI (Halle, 1954–5; also published separately, Halle, 1955).
2. A. H. Price, "Characterization in the *Nibelungenlied*," *Monatshefte*, Vol. LI (1959).
3. Bert Nagel, "Das Dietrichbild des Nibelungenliedes," *Zeitschrift für deutsche Philologie*, Vols. LXXVIII and LXXIX (1959–60).
4. H. Linke, "Über den Erzähler im *Nibelungenlied* und seine künstlerische Funktion," *Germanisch-Romanische Monatsschrift*, Vol. XLI, Neue Folge Vol. X (1960).
5. H. B. Willson, "Blood and Wounds in the *Nibelungenlied*," *Modern Language Review*, Vol. LV (1960).
6. F. R. Schröder, "Sigfrids Tod," *Germanisch-Romanische Monatsschrift*, Vol. XLI, Neue Folge Vol. X (1960).
7. J. K. Bostock, "The Message of the *Nibelungenlied*," *Modern Language Review*, Vol. LV (1960).
8. Heinrich Hempel, "Zur Datierung des *Nibelungenliedes*," *Zeitschrift für deutsches Altertum*, Vol. XC (1960–61).
9. Werner Schröder, "Die Tragödie Kriemhilts im *Nibelungenlied*," *Zeitschrift für deutsches Altertum*, Vol. XC (1960–61).

10. D. G. Mowatt, "Studies towards an Interpretation of the *Nibelungenlied*," *German Life and Letters*, New Series Vol. XIV (1961).

11. Hugh Sacker, "On Irony and Symbolism in the *Nibelungenlied*," *German Life and Letters*, New Series Vol. XIV (1961).

12. K. C. King, "The Message of the Nibelungenlied—a Reply," *Modern Language Review*, Vol. LVII (1962).

13. Werner Hoffmann, "Zur Situation der gegenwärtigen Nibelungenforschung," *Wirkendes Wort*, Vol. XII (1962).

14. Hugh Sacker, "The Message of the *Nibelungenlied* and the Business of the Literary Critic," *Modern Language Review*, Vol. LVIII (1963).

15. Werner Hoffmann, "Die englische und amerikanische Nibelungenforschung 1959–1962," *Zeitschrift für deutsche Philologie*, Vol. LXXXIV (1965).

F ▪ ORAL-FORMULAIC THEORY

The following works do not mostly deal directly with the *Nibelungenlied*, but provide some background and further references for those interested in considering the *Nibelungenlied* in the light of oral-formulaic theory (see above, pp. 19–21).

1. Mathias Murko, *La poésie populaire épique en Yougoslavie au début du XXe siècle* (Paris, 1929).

2. Milman Parry, *L'Epithète traditionnelle dans Homère* (Paris, 1928).

3. *Serbocroatian Heroic Songs*, collected by Milman Parry, edited and translated by A. B. Lord (2 vols., Cambridge, Mass. and Belgrade 1953–4).

4. A. B. Lord, *The Singer of Tales* (Cambridge, Mass., 1960).

5. F. P. Magoun, jr., "The Oral-Formulaic Character of Anglo-Saxon Narrative Poetry," *Speculum*, Vol. XXVIII (1953).

6. Michael J. Capek, "A Note on Oral Formulism in the *Nibelungenlied*," *Modern Language Notes*, Vol. LXXX (1965).

REFERENCES TO MIDDLE HIGH GERMAN WORKS

Line references to Middle High German works refer to the following editions:

Das Nibelungenlied, ed. K. Bartsch and H. de Boor (13th ed.), Wiesbaden, 1956.
Der arme Heinrich, ed. H. Paul (7th ed.), Halle, 1930.
Erec, ed. F. Bech (3rd ed.), Leipzig, 1893.
Iwein, ed. G. F. Benecke and K. Lachmann (2nd ed.), Berlin, 1843.
Minnesangs Frühling (abbrev. MSF), 30th ed., newly revised by C. von Kraus, Zürich, 1950.
Tristan, ed. F. Ranke, Berlin-Frankfurt, 1949.
Walther, ed. K. Lachmann (5th ed.), Berlin, 1875.

COMMENTARY

✑ COMMENTARY

3,1 ■ *triuten* does not refer specifically to any one sort of loving. It can, in context, mean "to caress" (661,3), or "to make physical love to" (655,1), and most occurrences in the text are in this semantic area; but on one occasion it clearly conveys "to love from a distance" (272,3). Any attempt to limit its meaning in the present instance would be misguided. We are told, with precise generality, that Kriemhilde was made for loving, whether active or passive. Sifrid, the next main character to be introduced, is credited with similar characteristics (26,4), and their subsequent careers show in what varied ways this capacity of theirs is developed (see note 22,4).

There is a similar lack of specificity about *minnen*, although its centre is less physical, more emotional than that of *triuten*. Mostly it is used for "spiritual love and disinterested affection" (e.g. 136,3), but it also occurs as the emotional counterpart of *triuten* (656,2), where the adjacent lines suggest "feel love for," the adjacent stanzas "make love to."

See also notes 659,4; 1250,3.

7,4 ■ This seems to imply that Dankrat was quite active in his youth and won personal honour (cf. Etzel's reported achievements, 1235,4). No such statement is anywhere made about his three sons, whose honour seems to be purely inherited, who have not seen much, if anything, of the outer world (79–82), and whose lands have never been attacked (158,4).

Gunther's position as preserver of a stagnant kingdom resembles that of Mark in Gottfried's *Tristan* (e.g. *Tristan* 437 ff. and 5927–30). There are, admittedly, advantages to this state of affairs. It makes for peace, security, and a civilized way of life. But this only holds good while reputation is taken for fact, and while the threat of greatness is strong enough to prevent its being challenged. For Sifrid, the reputation of the Burgundians constitutes a challenge in itself (cf. stanzas 53–55), and although they succeed in containing him for a while, the after-effects of the clash destroy everyone concerned. For Tristan, his uncle's court represents a lure which he can never give up (5634 ff.); the court accordingly survives in the long run better than he does.

Both heroes expose the hollowness of their hosts' pretensions when they save their adopted countries from disgrace (Sifrid the champion against the Saxons parallels Tristan the champion against Morolt). Neither Gunther nor Mark seem to mind this exposure; for such figureheads it is immaterial where their support comes from. But Mark's courtiers quickly break out into open envy and hatred of Tristan (8316 ff.), and Hagen later kills Sifrid.

See also notes 64,4; 115,4; 993.

12,1–4 ■ Even the desperate heroism of the Burgundians at the end of the work is no confirmation of the assertion made here, for by that time their court has ceased to exist, let alone to exercise any influence over its surroundings. In any case, there is something hollow and unconvincing about this stanza, with its defeatist formula ("No one could tell you all about . . ."), and the weak repetition of *kraft* in the first line. It may be possible to read some distinction into this (see Bartsch's note), but the repetition is there all the same.

It is, of course, true that similar defeatist formulae are often used with great effect in hyperbolic description, and can be classed together as a rhetorical device. When, as here, hyperbole is proved unjustified by events, the device, and indeed the whole orthodox description, may acquire a specific function in the work. (See Sacker, "On Irony and Symbolism in the *Nibelungenlied, German Life and Letters*, New Series Vol. XIV [1961].)

It is also true that the occurrence of such formulae throughout the *Nibelungenlied* can be used as evidence in the investigation of its genesis. This question, in particular the "Oral-formulaic" theory, is discussed in the Introduction, pp. 19-21. In general, the notes in this Commentary are not concerned with labelling the pieces, or tracing their origins, so much as with studying their possible function in the poem.

13,2 ▩ The dream foretells Sifrid's murder—rather ineptly, since there are few points of contact between Gunther's and Hagen's treachery on the one hand, and the attack of two eagles on the other. Kriemhilde's subconscious is much more accurate in her vision of the actual relationship between Sifrid and herself. She sees herself as training, or domesticating (*züge*), a wild animal, only to lose the finished product. From the Kürenberger's poem on the same subject (*MSF* 8, 33 ff.), we learn that it took about a year to get a falcon tamed just as you want him.[1] This may provide a background for the otherwise rather excessive time that Sifrid is kept hanging around for a glimpse of Kriemhilde. If a year or more is an accepted domesticating or screening period, then Sifrid's wait may be seen as part of the training process mentioned by Kriemhilde here. (See also note 105,2, for a discussion of *zuht*, and note 980,1.)

Apart from the training, however, the adjectives *starc*, *scoene* and *wilde* furnish a beautifully economic description of Sifrid's three essential characteristics. The strength and beauty are repeatedly mentioned; the wildness only shown in action. But it is this last quality that is most revealing, both for Kriemhilde's motives here, and for the whole Burgundian courtship and murder of Sifrid.

Note also that in the ancient Babylonian *Gilgamesh Epic*, which has many points of comparison with the *Nibelungenlied*, the Sifrid-like half-god, half-beast Enkidu is tamed by a woman – and then enters into a close (homosexual) relationship with the hero Gilgamesh. In the *Nibelungenlied*, of course, there is no exact equivalent to Gilgamesh, though possibly Hagen may initially

[1] Cf. A. T. Hatto, "Das Falkenlied des Kürenbergers," *Euphorion*, Vol. LIII (1959).

envisage establishing a not dissimilar relationship (see also notes 976, 2–3 and 993).

17,2–4 ▪ Kriemhilde knows her *Minnesang* (cf. Pseudo-Dietmar, *MSF* 39,24), and is quick to apply it to her own situation. Rather like the girl in *Der arme Heinrich*, she draws the conclusion that a blessing so mixed as love is better avoided altogether. In the event, of course, she fails to avoid it, and the narrator is able to echo her truism at the end (2378,4). By then, however, it has acquired an ironic flavour, as if all the intervening grandeur and catastrophe could still be reduced to Kriemhilde's terms. It also reminds us how little she has changed since the death of Sifrid, and how little she has understood of the events and developments since then. With everything destroyed, including even Kriemhilde herself, it is fitting to remember the small mind that started it all.[2]

19,4 ▪ Scattered throughout the work are references to the murder of Sifrid and the final destruction of the Burgundians. They remove all tension as to what will happen, and concentrate the interest on how and why it happens. At each point in the story the narrator pauses and invites his audience to reflect that this too is one element in a pattern whose totality is self-annihilation. (Burghart Wachinger's *Studien zum Nibelungenlied*, 1960, reviewed by D. G. Mowatt in *German Life and Letters*, New Series Vol. XIV [1961], p. 304, analyses the occurrence of these "anticipations" in interesting detail. See also above, p. 11.)

20,1–4 ▪ There is an obvious parallelism between this sketch of Sifrid's family, and the introduction of Kriemhilde, stanzas 2–4. Lines 2,1 and 20,1 (*Ez wuohs in Burgonden ein vil edel . . .; Do wuohs in Niderlanden eins edelen . . .*) are variants of the same formula, and predispose us to compare these two figures in their environments. In both cases we find a family resemblance between the names, which is broken by the central character (*Sifrid* as

_____

[2] J. K. Bostock, "The Message of the *Nibelungenlied*," *Modern Language Review*, Vol. LV (1960), p. 208, sees this stanza (17) as the first sign of Kriemhilde's arrogance and pride.

against *Sige-*, and Kriemhilde as against *G—*): a homogeneous setting with one misfit.

There are, of course, dissimilarities between the settings as well, in that Kriemhilde has a mother, three brothers and Hagen, while Sifrid has only a mother and father. This reinforces the impression of a central misfit, as the two families line up for courtship. Kriemhilde, the model of orthodox attractiveness, is lodged in the more complex, obscurely structured background. Sifrid, a most extraordinary suitor (cf. stanzas 87–100; 110), has the simplest possible family relationships.

21,4 ■ It is always difficult to assess the force of *hey!*, but one thing that it certainly does is draw attention to the sentiment of the line, in an elbow-nudging sort of way, as if approval were being sought. In the present case, it asks the reader to agree that the Burgundians Sifrid met at Gunther's court were as bold a bunch as you could find. Sifrid himself repeats this belief in stanzas 107–8, while making it clear that he has it only by hearsay. The actual reaction of Gunther's court (111–12) is cautious and diplomatic, rather than *snel*, and Sifrid is suitably disappointed in them. The overall effect of the line, then, is to emphasize the degree of faith which would be needed in order to believe the assertion contained in it.

22,2 ■ Hyperbolic expressions involving *wunder* are frequently used of courtly magnificence (food, dress, riches). With Sifrid, these expressions have another dimension, in that he actually has performed superhuman feats, and still can.

22,4; 24,4; 26,3–4 ■ From these three passages, it is evident that Sifrid is more experienced in love than either Kriemhilde or Brünnhilde. The precise quality of his experience is not specified, although *triuten* can refer to physical love-making, and this is certainly what Gunther has in mind when he warns Sifrid off his wife (655,1). Here, however, it is Sifrid's *success*, in any form of love, that is emphasized, together with the fact that he was well aware of his prowess in this field (24,4). Both these qualities, naïve success and naïve conceit, are central to Sifrid's character

as a fighting man. The realization that they extend to his character as a lover helps to clarify his blasé treatment of Brünnhilde,
and his casual dismissal of Kriemhilde (862). There is no need to
play down this aspect by insisting that *trûten* is subjunctive, or by
excluding the physical connotations of the word.
    See also note 3,1.

31,2 ▪ The second half of this line (*des newas niht rât*) is a recog-
nizable formula (cf. de Boor's note), but this fact does not determine interpretation. Whether it has any significance or not will
depend on its context, which in this case is unmistakably in favour of meaninglessness. The enjambement between stanzas 30 and
31 is usually taken as a sign of lateness; since the second of the
two stanzas adds very little to the first, it could also be taken as a
sign of feebleness. Even more striking (and not mentioned by
Bartsch or de Boor), is the poorness of the fourth line (31,4). The
second half of this line in B is impossible to scan (*da sin sun Sivrid
wol ritters namn gewan*), and neither Bartsch nor de Boor can
produce a very impressive line by their controlled eclecticism.
The overall impression given by the stanza, then, is one of
tedious and repetitive aimlessness.
    There still remains the question of how far this effect is func-
tional, if at all. One thing that can be said is that padding of this
sort is primarily found in scenes of courtly ceremonial, and
emphasizes, whether intentionally or not, the tediousness inherent in such recurrent rituals.

43,3–4 ▪ Both Bartsch and de Boor try to clarify this rather enigmatic passage by translating *für* as "in Abwehr von." De Boor
further explains Sifrid's ambition as a desire to protect his future
subjects against lawless violence.
    There are objections to this view. First, it strains the sense of
für, which normally means "in front of" or "above." There is no
verb of protecting here to give it the sense of "against"; instead,
the context selects in favour of "over" (*herre für* "lord over"),
"above" (*für allen den gewalt*; cf. *für elliu wîp* "above all
women," MSF passim), and "unthreatened by" (*des . . . vorhte
der degen*). Secondly, such a view finds little echo in Sifrid's char-

acter as we know it in the poem. And thirdly, it ignores the main emphasis of the passage, namely that Sifrid refuses crown and sceptre in order to prosecute this course of action, whatever it is. Sifrid himself explains his refusal to Gunther (see note 109) as a rejection of the outward show of authority in favour of a chance to prove his inherent capacity to rule. It is natural that Sifrid should be more interested in real power, at which he excels, than in the mechanics of government. It is also natural that he should fear such power wherever he sees it (line 4), and should try to gain control of it in some way. Compare his impatience with protocol in stanzas 315, 748, and 932.

The sense of *herre sîn für allen den gewalt*, then, is not specific, and may be close to what Sifrid understands by his all-embracing claim to Gunther in stanza 113,3: *ich wil es alles walten*, and again in stanza 122: *daz die hende mîn   wellent vil gewaltec hie zen Burgonden sîn.*
See also note 412,2.

47,1 ■ The phrase *hôhe minne* is common in Minnesang, and relates to carefully regulated love in high places, as against more casually contracted liaisons. In Minnesang, the educative and ennobling aspects of such relationships are generally stressed.

In the case of Sifrid's courtship of Kriemhilde, the elevated, public, serious side is there from the start, but the submission to all the rules and regulations of courtly love only comes after his first uncourtly overture is turned aside (stanza 110; contrast stanza 138).

In the case of Brünnhilde (stanza 544,4), it is difficult to see anything comparable to the behaviour of a "lady" in Minnesang. Kriemhilde, on the other hand, who applies the phrase to Brünnhilde, is a model of courtly inaccessibility. Since she in fact knows Brünnhilde's style of courtship, how different it is from her own, and how dangerous it could be for Gunther (stanza 544,3), it seems likely that she calls it *hôhiu minne* with ironic intent.

48,4 ■ Although Sifrid and Gunther behave correctly in selecting their wives according to general report, without personal acquaintance, they still make their choice to suit themselves rather than the needs of inter-state diplomacy. They may be concerned only with the type, and not with the individuality of the women of their choice, but the types they choose are nevertheless very revealing for their characters. Etzel, by contrast, does not even bother to choose for himself; what he requires is that his wife should be physically beautiful, and suitable as queen (stanza 1149). This is no doubt the more statesmanlike approach, and would have worked well if the woman he chose had not been Sifrid's widow. As it is, Rüdeger's doubts on this score are brushed rather rashly aside (stanzas 1157–8).

55,4 ◼ Even this early in the epic it is clear that Kriemhilde is by no means the only attraction for Sifrid at Worms (cf. 64,2–4). Equally important is the prospect of a good fight. By the time he arrives at the Burgundian court, he seems indeed to have forgotten about Kriemhilde altogether (107, 108), and echoes, almost in the same words, the boast he had made to his father (110,2–3).

The phrase (ich) trouwe . . .+infinitive seems characteristic of Sifrid's easy confidence in his own powers. In this case it also serves to smooth away his mother's justified forebodings, and shows up one of his more sympathetic sides: immediate sympathy and concern for any friend in trouble. The confidence and concern are still there when he uses the same phrase to Gunther (156,4; 174,4), but he shows a certain lack of respect for majesty by including Gunther's affairs of state in the same category as his mother's fears.

Apart from these three occurrences close together, the phrase (ich) trouwe . . .+ infinitive is used once each by Dankwart and Brünnhilde (514,2; 518,3), when they are arguing about who should spend her treasure, i.e. in a competitive context of claim and counter-claim. Dankwart struts, where Sifrid swaggers. Up to the death of Sifrid, only Hagen (873,2) and Gunther (638,3) also use this phrase, once each, and nicely differentiated. Hagen modifies his confidence with heinlîche, contrasting with Sifrid's bluff openness. (Sifrid's only qualification is wol 156,4; 174,4.) Gunther's qualification goes even further (naturally enough, since he is addressing his wife), and becomes a flat negation: ine trûwe iu . . . an gesigen.

Dankwart's hypothetical challenge to Sifrid (*ih trûte wol erstrîten* 117,3) and the narrator's interpretative comments on Sifrid's behaviour (*er trouwete niht erwerben* 320,2; *er trûwet wol erwerben* 424,4) reinforce the impression that this phrase belongs to Sifrid's world.

After Sifrid's death, only Hagen uses the phrase (1570,4; 1828,3). Both occurrences are in a context where Hagen is protecting, or taking responsibility for, the fate of the Burgundians. His position as ferryman (1570,4) is reminiscent of Sifrid on the way to Isenstein; his guarding of the sleeping men (1828,3) is reminiscent of Sifrid's single-handed prosecution of the Saxon war, while Gunther relaxes at home with the ladies. Even the dependent verbs are the same: (Sifrid) *ich trouwe iu wol behüeten* ... (174,4); (Hagen) *ich trûwe uns wol behüeten* ... (1828,3). This reminiscence is a nice reinforcement of the impression gained from the broader outlines of the plot, that Hagen in some sense takes over Sifrid's function after his death. Or perhaps it is just that he resumes his rightful place—in the open and at the centre.[3]

See also note 1783.

64,4 ■ Sifrid's curiosity about Kriemhilde is directed more to her environment than to her character. His father's warnings deal entirely with the rest of the family (stanzas 54–59), and Sifrid here seems to associate the problem directly with the number of men he should take with him. It is as if his journey were designed, at least partly, to find out what sort of feats a prospective suitor would have to perform (cf. 107). Kriemhilde thus appears as an excuse for him to measure himself against the Burgundians, rather than as an end in herself (a similar function to that of Enite in Erec's first combat). See also note 55,4. Sifrid certainly has no thought of staying at Worms longer than is necessary (76,4; 258).

87,4 ■ Sifrid belongs both in the courtly, rational world in which

[3] J. K. Bostock, "The Message of the *Nibelungenlied*," *Modern Language Review*, Vol. LV (1960), p. 206, believes Hagen is intentionally contrasted with Sifrid and comes off best in the comparison. In particular, Hagen is seen as "idealistic," "responsible" and "impeccably" loyal, whereas Sifrid is merely "charming" and driven by "self-interest."

he was educated, and in the primitive, irrational world of the
Nibelungs. To complain that these two worlds are not rationally
integrated is to miss the point; the ensuing complications largely
result from the impossibility of Sifrid's dual nature being contained by either world. It may be noted that only Hagen knows
about Sifrid's irrational world, and that even he appears quite out
of his depth when he visits it (406–7).

See also note 739,2.

99,4 ▪ Hagen sees Sifrid's feats as symptoms of his strength,
rather than as achievements in themselves. Sifrid himself takes a
similar attitude, in that he shows little interest in his treasure,
once gained, and even less in Brünnhilde, once overcome. (For
comparable elements in his attitude to Kriemhilde, see note 64,4.)
Both acquisitions are essentially accidents. In both cases, and even
in the slaying of the dragon (stanza 100), it is Sifrid's bravery,
strength and invulnerability that matter.

See also note 101.

101 ▪ The metrical emphasis of wir (line 1), stresses the shift from
the story of Sifrid's adventures to the conclusions that Hagen
draws from this story for the Burgundians. (See also note 99,4.)
The way he arrives at these conclusions shows something of
Hagen's limitations. Sifrid is invulnerable, therefore he should be
well received; he is brave and strong, therefore they should get
him on their side. It never occurs to his conscious mind that a man
with such superlative qualifications might turn out to be an
embarrassment (but see note 993).

105,2 ▪ The basic sense of zuht is "education," and it frequently
occurs throughout the Nibelungenlied in such phrases as maget-
lîcher zühte (414,2), and in riterlîchen zühten (371,3), with the
meaning "showing the marks of a well-trained, accomplished
courtly lady or gentleman." But the underlying connotation of
"something learned, with greater or lesser difficulty" is only dor-
mant, and can be brought out at any time by the context. In the
present example, the surrounding phrase in vil wenec iht gebrast
suggests an examination successfully passed, and the emphasis is
on correctness of behaviour: "they were careful not to put a foot

wrong." The effort was clearly worthwhile, since it extorts a similar politeness from Sifrid (105,3-4) and sets up a framework of reference for the whole encounter which he is reluctantly forced to accept (127).

The singular form *zuht* frequently has much the same meaning, "polished, courtly behaviour," but it also occurs in contexts where the sense of "restraint, instruction, correction" is apparent (cf. *Walther* 87,1–2: *nieman kan mit gerten/ kindes zuht beherten* and *Der arme Heinrich* 120: *die swaeren gotes zuht,* both of which refer to corrective measures, possibly physical; *Iwein* 1056: *her Iwein jagete in âne zuht* "without restraint.") See also note 13,2. These connotations are certainly present in the singular *zuht* of 497,4, and probably in the plural *zühte* of 496,4 as well.

107 ▪ See note 64,4.

109 ▪ Sifrid is referring to his rejection of his father's earlier offer (see note 43,3–4). "I'm a warrior too, and they wanted to put the crown on my head, but I want to prove my worth first."

113,3 ▪ See note, 43,3–4.

115,4 ▪ Compare 109,3.

Two concepts of the right to rule (*reht*) are opposed in this scene. The traditional, conservative and impersonal attitude of the Burgundians is summed up by Gunther (stanza 112). The experimental and intensely individual approach of Sifrid comes out in his challenge to Gunther, as well as his refusal to accept the right to rule as a gift from his father (43,1–4). The contrast is underlined by the fact that the lone Sifrid has to confront three kings, with their advisors. Instead of inciting an individual to face him, he has to take on the whole court.

Since the challenge and the whole wooing of Kriemhilde are part of this self-justification that Sifrid demands, it seems surprising that he should eventually accept Kriemhilde as a gift from Gunther. Admittedly he performs two feats in order to qualify, but neither is directly related to winning her. One of them indeed is a procedure carefully designed for the winning of someone else. By then he has moved a long way from his original attitude, and towards the Burgundian position. He now seems to believe, as they do, that: (1) Gunther has a right to be king, because his father was king before him, and because he has done nothing to disqualify himself; (2) Gunther has a right to Brünnhilde because he is king; and (3) Sifrid's undeniable superiority, both at fighting and at wife-winning, must be used against the Saxons and Brünnhilde to create the illusion of its own non-existence.

See also note 7,4.

118 ■ It is noticeable that Sifrid (here) and Brünnhilde (especially in stanza 821) are more conscious of rank than is anyone else in the *Nibelungenlied*. At Worms everyone knows his place, and these things never need to be referred to. Sifrid and Brünnhilde seem unable to accept a status tacitly upheld by the system. They both need to assert their own positions.

119,3 ■ Gunther's dependence on Hagen comes out clearly here, although the precise nature of the dependence at this moment is obscure. It may be that Hagen is always relied on to take the initiative, or it may be that Gunther is more than usually at a loss after Hagen's display of inside knowledge about Sifrid (stanzas 87–103). Whatever his function may have been earlier, it is certain that the arrival and absorption of Sifrid put him into the position of mediator, rather than ultimate resource (see note 193,1–2). From now on, the Burgundians follow him in everything to do with Sifrid, up to and including his murder and the disposal of the treasure. On other matters (Kriemhilde's second marriage; the journey to Hunland), his advice is ignored (see notes 1078,3 and 1204,3).

There is no direct evidence that Hagen resents his relegation, if that is what it is, but he does murder Sifrid with some relish when the time comes, and seems to reassert himself as a second Sifrid later. See notes 863,4. 1572,3–4; 1657,3.

121,3–4 ■ For a possible function for Hagen's use of the third person, see note 965–8.

122,4 ■ See note 43,3–4.

126,1 ■ Gunther, Gernot and Giselher are only to a limited extent
treated as separate individuals in the *Nibelungenlied*; often they
function rather as different aspects of the same multivalent figure-
head, of which now one aspect, now another comes to the fore.
Gunther poses in general as diplomatic and dignified, Giselher as
friendly and forthcoming (see note 1078,3). Gernot, the one in
the middle, tends to prepare the way for whichever of his brothers
is about to hold the stage, and on occasion at the point of transition may even merge, as here, with the brother in question. This
merging of identity has caused scholars much unnecessary worry
(cf. note 2188,1).

127,4 ■ The persistent courtesy of Gunther and Gernot has
triumphed over the warmongering elements in both Sifrid's
character and the Burgundian court (119–125). This is just one
instance of how the courtly "padding" of the first part of the
Nibelungenlied is functional. In the second half of the poem,
Hagen and Volker on the one side, and Kriemhilde on the other,
manage to prevent a similar accord from developing between
Etzel and the Burgundian kings—and so the dreary but peaceful
ceremonial which obtains at Gunther's court never properly un-
folds at Etzel's, but is replaced by short stormy scenes leading to
war.
  See also note 129,3.

129,3 ■ The narrator's protestation of truthfulness inevitably
draws attention to his assertion *daz het versolt sîn ellen*, and raises
the question of what, if anything, it might mean. In one sense it is
a straight lie: far from being allowed to gain honour in Burgundy
by proving his *ellen*, Sifrid saw his challenge rejected, and was
forced instead to accept the friendship and hospitality offered. In
another sense, however, the respect and affection shown him are
due to his bravery and strength. The ambiguity arises because the
Burgundians are quite happy to take these qualities on hearsay, as
adornments to the court, whereas Sifrid can only conceive of them
in action. These two divergent attitudes to virtue are at the root
of Sifrid's whole impossibility and death. Sifrid is driven to un-

necessary actions (the second fight with Alberich, the presentation of ring and girdle to Kriemhilde, flamboyant excellence at the hunt), because this is how he shows what he is. The Burgundians are forced to kill him precisely because he is the embodiment of their ideals. But as long as they remain ideals, subscribed to but never put to the test, all Sifrid's qualities can be tolerated, even encouraged at Worms. Even his ability to fulfil Brünnhilde's antisocial demands has its devitalized Burgundian equivalent: in the festivities mentioned in the next stanza, he excels (130,2) at precisely those games which courtship of Brünnhilde requires (130,4; cf. stanza 327).

135,4 ■ See note 3,1.

138,3 ■ Kriemhilde's extraordinary seclusion—and for that matter her general subservience to her brothers—is peculiar to her and may be used as evidence for her character and for that of the Burgundian court. Brünnhilde, by contrast, comes out to challenge suitors on her own account; Rüdeger's daughter is as subservient to her father as is Kriemhilde to her brothers, but she is not secluded.

Both Sifrid and Kriemhilde are extremes, and their uneasy liaison is a model of incompatibility. Kriemhilde the untouchable gets casually beaten by her husband. Sifrid the irresistible waits on Kriemhilde for a year without even being allowed to see her. Nowhere is it suggested that either of the partners benefited in the slightest from the acquisition of such uncharacteristic behaviour patterns.

The only people who benefit (for the moment) from the stalemate between Sifrid and Kriemhilde are the Burgundians. It takes an intrusion from outside, in the shape of the Saxons, to move things on. The pattern "stalemate achieved, then broken into from outside" is recurrent at Worms, e.g.

(1) peace broken into by Sifrid's arrival;

(2) stalemate between Sifrid and Kriemhilde broken by Saxons;

(3) peace between Worms and Santen broken by Brünnhilde's uneasiness;

(4) stalemate between the kings and Kriemhilde broken by Etzel's offer of marriage;

(5) peace between Burgundy and Hunland broken by Kriemhilde's invitation.

See also note 715,2.

142,4 ■ Gunther's behaviour throughout this scene is unexceptionable. In successfully protecting his country from attack, he excels as a diplomatic monarch. Sifrid is made to bear the brunt of the fighting, and Burgundian losses are reduced to a minimum. Gunther stays at home, putting the good of the state before any personal ambition for death-or-glory as a warrior (cf. stanza 174). Since his more fearsome aspect is so much in eclipse at the moment, this sudden reference to *der grimme Gunther*, and to the terror he inspires in all messengers, undermines confidence in the adequacy of conventional formulae to every situation. Its irrelevance to this particular situation is brought out by the immediately preceding description of Gunther the smiling diplomat (*gruozte scône* 142,1; cf. *der künec guot* 147,1). Two opposing clichés of kingship are played off against each other, each one showing the other up. By its very extremity, this reference to the heroic Gunther helps to focus attention on his unheroic behaviour. The latter is in any case well documented in this scene; cf. stanza 147,1–2; and note 152.

150,2 ■ This fatalism of the fighting-man is often claimed as something peculiar to the Germanic tribes in the "heroic" period. Perhaps this period was unusual in having no set of official euphemisms for the realities of war, but the attitude of the men involved hardly seems to have changed. In the wars of 1914–18, and 1939–45, fatalistic phrases such as: "his number's up," and "he's had his lot" were used as a defence against official heroism.

151,4 ■ Twelve weeks (145,1) would doubtless have seemed long enough to Hagen, as to the others, had he been content to use the Burgundian forces; elsewhere (e.g. 339,4; 1473–82) one does not get the impression that assembling an army takes so very long. But Hagen, both here and in the wooing of Brünnhilde (331), is anxious to exploit Sifrid's strength and desire for Kriemhilde to

the greater glory of the Burgundian court; and even after Sifrid's
death Hagen adopts a similar attitude to what is left of Sifrid's
power, the treasure (1107; cf. 774,4).
   See also notes 993; 1031.

152 ▪ If this stanza is printed without brackets around the
phrase: *daz was wol getân* (cf. de Boor's edition), the calculating
and unheroic side of Gunther becomes very obtrusive. The
brackets select in favour of a translation such as: "he ordered the
messengers to be well looked after while he clarified his position."
Without the brackets, it is most natural to read line 4 as directly
dependent on *daz was wol getân*, giving the reading: "he was
well advised to treat them nicely until he knew how much support he had." The juxtaposition of this real powerlessness with
the cliché *Gunther der rîche* (line 3) would then have a function
similar to that discussed in note 142,4.

155–56 ▪ Sifrid is very susceptible to requests for help (see note
748,1–2). By the time they want to murder him, the Burgundians
know this and can use it unscrupulously (875). More surprisingly,
it is apparent from the striking similarity of the technique employed by Gunther on both occasions (compare stanzas 153–4
with 883) that he has at least an intuitive knowledge of Sifrid's
weakness from the start. The only difference between the present
situation and the later one is that Gunther is not yet certain of
Sifrid's position; or perhaps he is certain, and wants Sifrid to make
it explicit. At all events, his throwing up of the category *staeten
vriwenden* (155,3) for Sifrid to catch is skilful and effective.

156,4 ▪ See note 55,4.

161,4 ▪ See note 343,4.

174,1–3 ▪ See note 886,1.

174,4 ▪ See note 55,4.

181,1–2 ▪ Here, as in 88,1, *helfe* can be taken in its usual sense
of "help." The phrase *wider sîner helfe* would then mean something like "against his helping hand."

193,1–2 ▪ By giving the *gewalt* to Sifrid (see note 43,3–4), and by describing Hagen as *Guntheres man*, these lines again emphasize Hagen's function as mediator. See note 119,3.

194 ▪ Sifrid takes an inhuman satisfaction in blood and slaughter throughout this scene. Cf. 181,4; 206,3, where *sînen muot ervollen* is the operative phrase.

See also note 230,3–4.

209 ▪ This stanza fits only loosely into its context. Stanzas 198–217 convey (1) that there was a general mêlée in which Sifrid was outstanding, and (2) that when Liudeger discovered for certain that Sifrid was his opponent, he immediately gave in. Stanza 209 comes in the middle, and seems to state that Liudeger knew even at this stage that Sifrid must be responsible. This "knowledge" could perhaps be explained as inner conviction, following on a rumour of Sifrid's possible participation (168,3), but it would be a mistake to insist on integrating it too rationally with the rest.

Cf. note 1010,4.

230,3–4 ▪ The juxtaposition is bald; the most out and out knightly description of Sifrid, straight after an account of his most bloody exploits. *küene* is well enough prepared, but *guot . . . an allen tugenden* comes as something of a shock, and underlines the paradox that it is precisely Sifrid's virtues that make him so terrible to the Burgundians (see also note 129,3). The two lines taken together emphasize the similarities as well as the differences between Sifrid the blood-soaked warrior and Sifrid the bashful suitor. His performance in both fields is hyperbolic; a year at Burgundy without even *seeing* Kriemhilde is an extreme application of *Minnedienst* conventions, just as winning the Saxon war single-handed is an extreme example of valour.

258,1 ▪ Sifrid is restless in Burgundy (cf. 76,4; 320), and only held there by the diplomatic dangling of Kriemhilde (258,4; 138,3; 289). In view of this and his earlier extreme confidence (stanzas 55–9), it is surprising that he now takes his leave without ever mentioning Kriemhilde. The fact that he does so is a great achievement for the Burgundians. He is so far removed from his original intention of taking her alone, by storm, that the glimpse he is now offered takes the form of a routine public appearance for all the assembled knights. And even this is suggested by Ortwin (stanzas 273–4).

259,1 ▪ The theme of the independent helper comes up again with the ferryman that Hagen kills (see also note 1572,3–4). The rather close parallel (both figures are too important and independent to accept payment, both act as ferryman without considering it their main profession, both are killed by Hagen), suggests that one of Sifrid's crimes may be his unemployability. He helps the Burgundians out of the goodness of his heart, and not because he owes it to them.

287,4 ▪ See note 105,2.

289 ▪ See note 258,1.
    This speech of Gernot's is the most blatant formulation of the Burgundian attitude towards Sifrid. It is also the most revealing of the function of Kriemhilde's seclusion (see note 138,3). However she may explain her compulsive virginity to herself (17), it is clear that her brothers regard it as a marketable commodity. For them, the kiss allowed in stanza 297 is nothing but a political act. For Sifrid and Kriemhilde, of course, it is much more (cf. 294,4; 295), but the Burgundians are reluctant to believe that Kriemhilde might have emotions other than those they themselves prescribe for her. They make the same mistake when they allow her to marry Etzel (1204), and then accept her invitation to Etzel's court (1460–62). To them, she is their sister, and nothing more (1204; 1131).

296 ▪ Similar earthy sentiments are expressed as the occasion arises by Gunther (stanza 625) and Etzel (see note 1358,3–4), but not by Sifrid. Admittedly, Sifrid's behaviour at the moment (e.g. 296,4; 285) may be classed as uncharacteristic, but even in his element (e.g. at Isenstein) his mouth never waters.

302–303 ■ The superiority of Sifrid, obvious enough in the Saxon war, is here openly accepted by Kriemhilde, as it was by Sifrid himself (174). They both appear to assume that Sifrid can draw to himself the loyalty of Gunther's men without disturbing the peace at court. When one thinks of Kriemhilde's later success in the raising of a substitute army, and of Hagen's reaction (1128), the complacent insolence of this pair of lovers begins to look ominous. The otherwise sugary conformism of their behaviour only serves to heighten the contrast.

304 ■ The Burgundians' plan to make Sifrid into their chief supporter (see notes 101, 155–56 and 289) has succeeded. His pretended vassalage (386,3) illustrates both his enthusiasm for, and his detachment from, this role—which is also the one invoked by Hagen to lure him to his death (874–75).

310 ■ We usually say that Gunther is being polite and courtly here; he is, but there is something very correct and strained about his performance, especially when the previous stanza is considered. It is this sort of behaviour that confuses Sifrid when he first arrives. In any case, the rigid pattern breaks down four stanzas later, where Sifrid shows a natural generosity in startling contrast (see note 315). As always, there is something superior, faintly contemptuous, about Sifrid's attitude to the rules made for lesser men.

315 ■ This act of Sifrid's is one of the many ways in which he puts himself outside the courtly circles at Worms. Gunther (314) is utterly correct, as always. Sifrid has no interest in propriety. His generosity here is as cavalier as the butchery he has just completed. Liudeger (298) is well aware of Sifrid's entirely personal, non-political and terrifyingly simple motives. Sifrid later shows a similar generosity to Alberich (see note 496,4), and one commentator (de Boor, note) claims both acts as examples of chivalric orthodoxy. The contrast with Gunther in the first case, and the whole unknightly atmosphere in the second, argue strongly against such a framework.

320 ■ See note 258,1.

329 ■ The clichés seem more homogeneous and more cumulative
here than is usual in the *Nibelungenlied*, and for a moment
Gunther is very convincing in the role of all-or-nothing lover.
The contrast with his reactions in the event (stanza 442) is correspondingly more shocking, or amusing.
    See also notes 332–3; 655,4.

330 ■ Sifrid's detachment from Brünnhilde's way of life springs
directly from his attempt to see things from Gunther's point of
view. In fact, these "vreislîche sit" are made to measure for Sifrid
himself, as he later shows in Isenstein. His indifference to Brünnhilde and his friendly contempt for Gunther show up rather
bleakly after Gunther's inflated rhetoric in 329. It is difficult not
to feel sorry for Brünnhilde in advance, when we think how her
wares, so carefully preserved and laid out for Sifrid, will be
casually rejected and handed on to this pretentious figure-head
Gunther. Charity is conspicuously lacking in everyone but Sifrid
and Brünnhilde, and here Sifrid is doing his best to deny it.

331,4 ■ Sifrid's and Brünnhilde's knowledge of each other, which
has been made much of in genetical studies, is an essential part of
them, and no explanation is offered or required. The relationship
of Hagen to Etzel, on the other hand, has no function in the work,
and receives a correspondingly careful explanation (1756).
    See also note 378.

332–333 ■ A contrast is noticeable between Gunther's rhetorical
protestations (especially 332,4) and Sifrid's very practical terms
(stanza 333).
    See also notes 329; 388.

336,1 ■ The word *muose* is interesting. It emphasizes the negative
side of the *tarnkappe*, as against its more expansive connotations.
In one sense, it confers magical powers and fulfils infantile omni-
potence fantasies. But in another, it is a level of disguise and
deceit that Sifrid is *forced* to descend to in his dealings with Brünn-

hilde. (The only other times he wears the disguise are (1) his brief visit to Nibelunge and (2) his night in Gunther's bed, but again, in both cases, it is Brünnhilde he wishes to deceive; cf. stanzas 482; 509). The fact that the Brünnhilde escapade requires deceit from Sifrid, while the Saxon war does not, underlines the unique character of this particular service to Gunther. The Saxon war was a political challenge, and Sifrid's help was only what might have been expected of a vassal. Brünnhilde's challenge, however, relates directly to Gunther's private person, so that the politically legitimate procedure of delegation is no longer enough. Instead, a full impersonation, and therefore deceit, is demanded.

343,4 ■ The use of one's own name in this unsophisticated form is confined to Kriemhilde (four times: 355,4; 698,2; 1056,4; 1080,4) and Gunther (once: 343,4). The effect might be described as one of ego-inflation, and fits the overall tendency of Gunther and Kriemhilde to take on more than they can handle.

For other characters, the nearest approach is Rumold's: *welt ir niht volgen Hagene, iu raetet Rûmolt* (1466,1), where the self-reference in the second half of the line is rhetorically supported by a more normal usage in the first. It seems likely that some sort of comic effect is admissible here, from the discrepancy between Rumold's humble function and grandiose self-styling, and also quite simply from the juxtaposition of two such ill-assorted names. His advice, in the event, is hardly serious, and the whole effect recalls an earlier stanza (777), where Rumold was built up as a parody of the king-figures in the main plot.

Metonymic phrases of the pattern *diu Sîfrides hant, den Dietrîches lîp* are frequent in the *Nibelungenlied*, and occasionally we find a character talking about himself in this way. The effect is still grandiose, as when Rüdeger finally gives in to Kriemhilde, and says: *ez muoz hiute gelten der Rüedegêres lîp* (2163,2), although in Rüdeger's case the inflation is reluctant (see note 2163,2). This is the only example of the use of one's own name with *lîp*. When *hant* is substituted for *lîp*, we find four occurrences: one from Dietrich, and three from Sifrid. The phrase *diu Dietrîches hant* occurs only twice in the whole work (1902,4; 2361,1), and the occurrence with self-reference (1902,4) is in fact a *refusal* of help to Kriemhilde (*Sîfrit ist ungerochen von der Dietrîches hant*). Dietrich's desire for neutrality is thus reflected here. Sifrid, on the other hand, is characteristically and extravagantly helpful, and, as might be expected, the phrase *diu Sîfrides hant* is very frequently found (seventeen times in all), in contexts where his strong right arm is offered as protection. The proportion of self-referential occurrences, (three out of eighteen), is not all that high, and two out of the three are spoken to Gunther with intent to soothe (161,4; 884,4). The phrase *diu Rüedegeres hant* also occurs quite frequently (seven times, never with self-reference), but the aspect is the "open hand," or compulsive generosity of Rüdeger. Against this background, the three occurrences of *diu Guntheres hant* are pointedly ironic (472,3; 523,4; cf. 633,1). All these are in the context of Gunther's pseudo-conquest of Brünnhilde, and emphasize the pseudo-strongman side of Gunther throughout the episode.

In general it needs to be accepted that the formulae found so abundantly in the *Nibelungenlied* can sometimes be very subtly differentiated in their effects.

346 ■ It is slightly disturbing to find Hagen concerned about such matters. Although the issue is important, it is not really in his line. This may be due to his relegation now that Sifrid has become chief helper. On the other hand, he may be suggesting that Gunther should grow up (cf. Gurnemanz's advice to Parzival, [*Parzival*, lines 170, 10–14]); or simply reminding Gunther that Kriemhilde is grown up, and intimately concerned, via Sifrid, in the plans.

At Santen, it was Sifrid's mother who saw to the clothes (stanza 63). Nobody queried this, and in general, the level of fussiness and pomposity was much lower there (cf. note 771,3).

355,4 ■ See note 343,4.

356,1 ■ Kriemhilde's insistence (unparalleled in the poem) on her submissiveness may be correlated with her self-imposed isolation (17,4) and inaccessibility (133,4). In this sense, one might want to call her repressed, and to interpret her later fury as the characteristic break-down of a persona based on too savagely in-hibited desires. There is another sense, however, in which all her behaviour can be seen as goal-directed provocation. In the present scene, she asks to be ordered about. She next incites her husband to beat her, and then brags about it afterwards (894). By this same indiscretion to Brünnhilde she sets the stage for her hus-band's murder, and then gives Hagen the means to do it. After her ostentatious generosity with the Nibelung treasure, Hagen is forced to remove it from her. And finally, the monumental ex-tremity of her successive demands at the end is a virtual invitation for someone to kill her. It is as if she were masochistically deter-mined to turn her childish cynicism (17) into fact.

As far as the immediate effect of her attitude on Gunther is concerned, it seems that he actually needed the advice. He addresses her formally at first, as *ir* (350,1), then changes to *du* (354,2), apparently misled by the warmth of her welcome (351). Exhorted to show a little more kingly arrogance, he reverts to *ir* (357). He suffers a similar injection of regal back-bone from Brünnhilde (726–33), when she forces him to give orders to Sifrid. If these scenes are not to be taken as pure farce, they must point to one of the main threads of the work: the shifting relation between real and pretended power.

See also note 678,1.

360,3 ■ The importance attached to clothes at this point finds no echo at Isenstein. Brünnhilde's clothes are impressive in an un-expected sort of way (434 ff.), and the Burgundians do manage to hold their own (408). But all this is nothing in comparison with the trouble devoted to their preparation, or the fulsome tributes paid them before they set out (370).

If they do leave Brünnhilde's territory *âne scande*, it is not because of their finery, nor even because of their armour, both of which Brünnhilde treats with contempt (446–7), but solely be-cause of Sifrid.

378 ■ In this passage (cf. also 382,4; 384; 393; 407) Sifrid's affinity to Brünnhilde comes out very strongly. He belongs in Isenstein, and everyone accepts this fact, but it occurs to no one

to ask whether he has been there before. His familiarity with the place is part of the "homecoming" symbol, which draws its strength from the emotions connected with childhood, or even earlier, recollections. Evidently the yearning is basic enough to dispense with plot mechanics or history (cf. Mr. Polly and his pub, or the Jews and their promised land).

See also note 331,4.

385–6 ■ Possibly a single, rather hesitant, sentence runs right through from 385,2 to 386,3; this would give additional emphasis to Sifrid's hesitation in coming out with his surprising proposal. "Knowing" as he does about Isenstein, Sifrid presumably anticipates that Brünnhilde will hail him and not Gunther as her suitor. He therefore prepares to have an agreed explanation ready—to ensure her deception.

388 ■ This stanza makes it brutally clear that Sifrid regards his conquest of Brünnhilde as a direct service to Kriemhilde. Together with his Saxon war exploits and his prolonged love-sickness, the present adventure is a form of *Minnedienst*, and a way to Kriemhilde's courtly heart. We already know (289) that this is part of a Burgundian plot to use Kriemhilde as bait. All the same, it is ironical and a little naïve of Sifrid to offer his affinity with Brünnhilde as a qualification for his candidacy to Kriemhilde. No wonder that the bear, so long chained up and forced to dance for the Burgundians, should be let out just before he dies.

396,4–397,4 ■ The personal and reflexive use of *dunken* is neutral in the *Nibelungenlied*, occurring (apart from here) twice with ironic implications (447,3; 2327,1), and once in all seriousness (396,4). The undoubtedly ironic effect of line 396,4 comes perhaps from the scene in which it is embedded, where Gunther's pretensions so far outrun his true worth that even his own supporters are embarrassed (438; 443; 450).

By claiming so much for Sifrid's action, the line also invites us to wonder what was the real significance of this horse-holding ceremony or "service" (397,4). In one way it implies quite simply that Sifrid is Gunther's vassal. But the emphasis remains on Sifrid, and on the fact that a great man such as this was willing to subordinate himself to Gunther in order to increase the latter's worth. If this were not so, Gunther would have no cause to feel "enhanced," and Brünnhilde and her ladies would not have singled Sifrid out for greeting (411–419), in spite of having seen the whole thing (396). It is Sifrid's service, not Gunther's power which sticks in the mind. And it is the failure of this play-acting to convince Brünnhilde that leaves her permanently obsessed with Sifrid.

On the more purely sexual significance of Sifrid's holding Gunther's horse for him, compare 459,1 and 461,2, where Sifrid's reluctance to penetrate Brünnhilde complements his present eagerness that Gunther should. An additional farcical aspect of this horse-play is brought out when Sifrid actually *carries* Gunther himself (464,4).

406 ◼ Burgundian weapons are neither a protection nor a threat at Isenstein (see note 447,2). Much later, at Etzel's court, when Sifrid is dead and Brünnhilde reduced to nothing, Hagen's reluctance to surrender his arms is both fitting and practical, and Kriemhilde is far from smiling (stanza 1747).

412,2 ◼ The description of Gunther in this stanza is strangely qualified and muted. The others are all praised for some innate quality which the observer can see. Sifrid is just Sifrid (411), Hagen is terrible-looking (413) and Dankwart is young and beautiful (414–5). Gunther's attributes, on the other hand, are all hypothetical, and the proviso *ob er gewalt des hête*, if it is to mean anything at all, suggests once again the discrepancy between real and pretended power which runs through the whole work, but is particularly obtrusive in this scene. Could this maid of Brünnhilde's be referring to the same sort of *gewalt* that Sifrid meant in stanza 43? If so, then the surface irony, by which we know that Gunther is in fact a *künic rîch*, while the maid is still guessing, acquires another dimension. To Sifrid and Brünnhilde, Gunther is indeed someone without real power. By offering him the opportunity to prove his right to rule (113–14), Sifrid was giving him a chance to remedy this defect. We know that he refused. Again, Brünnhilde's maid, in not knowing this, is at a disadvantage, but so are we, in knowing it. Her description of the others is spontaneous reaction to their appearance. Why should this not hold true for Gunther as well? Perhaps, in the last resort, the irony is against us, and Gunther does just look like a mighty king with the power missing. He is eventually *given* power in Isenstein, on the strength of his supposed victory over Brünnhilde (*si erloubte im daz er solde haben dâ gewalt* 468,3), but he never makes use of it.

416,1 ■ *gewant* is nicely ambiguous (cf. 446,2 and 447,3, where the context clearly selects in favour of "armour"). Brünnhilde's ladies first clothe her in courtly dress, and then, after she has spoken with the Burgundians, in her armour. The latter seems the more appropriate to the Queen of Isenstein, but she is no more *totally* magical and primitive than is Sifrid. The co-existence of her womanly and unwomanly sides is underlined by the ambiguity of words such as *gewant*, and the juxtaposition of such words as *vreislîch* and *minneclîch* (see note 425,4).

More fundamentally, the whole scene compels us to realize that "womanly and unwomanly" are just two ways of looking at one thing. Brünnhilde's bellicosity (and eventual defeat) is an image of her attractiveness (and the result). Her *vreislîche sit* (330,2) are her way of being *minneclîch*, and a highly successful way it is. The Burgundians can react with horror, and Sifrid can react with half-guilty understanding (459). Brünnhilde herself is remarkably consistent, and even in her last fight in the bed the ambiguity persists. Her *hemde sô blanc* (670,2) is just an article of clothing to Gunther, and its removal a preliminary to sexual activity. But to Brünnhilde it is a defense, and she fights to preserve it. Similarly, her virginal girdle is an offensive weapon (636; 677), or a love token (680; 849–50).

Sifrid shows a similar identification of martial and erotic, and there are at least two verbal recollections of his behaviour in this scene. In 440,4, for example, the description of Brünnhilde's sword recalls that of Balmung 73,4, and in 434,2 *sam ob si solde strîten umb elliu küneges lant* is exactly how Sifrid begins his courtship of Kriemhilde (e.g. 113,3).

425,4 ■ The use of the adjective *minneclîch* here—where one might rather expect *vreislîch* (cf. 330,2)—emphasizes that it is precisely Brünnhilde's Amazonian characteristics which attract her suitors, and in view of Gunther's almost immediate reaction (442), the effect is rather ironic. The use of this word also contrasts Brünnhilde with Kriemhilde, *diu minneclîche* par excellence (242,1), while at the same time equating their functions. Both, after all, in their different ways, are asking to be beaten, and both are only partly satisfied in the event.

See also note 416,1.

434,2 ■ See note 416,1.

438,4; 442,2; 450,4 ■ Apart from the unheroic and farcical side of these reactions to Brünnhilde, they show Hagen and Gunther agreed on something quite serious and real. Brünnhilde, they are realising, is not for them, or for their world. For the moment, they unconsciously equate Sifrid with the Devil, as being something alien. When the equation becomes more obvious in Hagen's mind, he gets rid of him (with Gunther, even then, still trying not to recall his moment of truth).

From this point of view, the agreement between Gunther and Sifrid has something of a Faustian pact. The Burgundians sell their collective soul for extra power, and then try to escape their fate by having their Mephisto assassinated. But the final payment is still exacted by Kriemhilde, the *vâlandinne* in their midst.

See also note 1394,1.

440,4 ■ See note 416,1.

442 ■ See note 329.

447,2 ■ Brünnhilde, who seldom smiles, is remarkably unimpressed by the thought of the grim Hagen and the bold Dankwart, armed to the teeth. Their virility, on whatever level, is of no interest to her. Contrast the consternation of the courtly Kriemhilde, when she is confronted by Hagen, flaunting his sword in stanza 1783. Admittedly it is Sifrid's weapon he flaunts,

but the fact remains that Hagen armed is a threat to any man
but Sifrid, and a provocation to any woman but Brünnhilde.

For Brünnhilde's attitude to *gewant*, see notes 360,3 and 416,1.
For *(er)smielen* as against *lachen*, see note 709,1.

454,3 ▪ This is one of several remarks by Sifrid which sum up a
whole relationship in one image. It immediately recalls 174,3, also
to Gunther: *belîbet bî den frouwen   und traget hôhen muot*.
Similarly pregnant is 459,1 about Brünnhilde: *er dâhte: ich wil
niht schiezen   daz schoene magedîn*, and line 862,3 about
Kriemhilde and Brünnhilde: *verbiut ez dînem wîbe,   der
mînen tuon ich sam*. All Sifrid's relationships are direct, un-
adorned, unanalysed, and unformulated except in symbols.

459–461 ▪ See notes 396,4; 416,1; 454,3.

This refusal to penetrate Brünnhilde is symptomatic of Sifrid's
whole negligent conquest. Brünnhilde's reaction (461,2) is
pathetic, in that she is twice deceived—first, in thinking it is
Gunther and secondly, in thinking this is the real thing, the shock
she has been living for. Not only is she foisted off onto Gunther
after conquest, but the conquest itself is counterfeit. Neither here
nor later in bed does she experience the full force of Sifrid, the
spear sharp end first. The essential continuity between these two
unsatisfactory experiences is brought out again in stanza 820,3–4.
(See also note 820, 3–4).

468,1–3 ▪ There is an element of irony in the emphasis put here
on Gunther's *tugent* (in the sense of courtesy); what is required
of him in the encounter with Brünnhilde is not so much *tugent* as
kraft—which he lacks, as the preceding line indicates. His earlier
lack of *gewalt* is also emphasized in line 3, in that he now re-
receives power as a gift from Brünnhilde.

See also note 412,2.

472,3 ▪ See note 343,4.

482 ▪ In Nibelunge, the realm of pure magic and brute strength,
Sifrid can give free rein to that side of his nature which he has

been suppressing at Worms: he fights Alberich and the others unnecessarily, almost for the fun of it. But in consequence they jump to do what he commands—no council is necessary here (501–503). The contrast with the complexities of Worms is clear (compare 500,3 with 109,3 and 115,4; or 488,1 with 109,1), but so is that with the weakness of Gunther at Isenstein (compare 500,2 with 454,3).

There is a parallel contrast between the brusque "no-nonsense" atmosphere here and the weary proliferation of court ceremonial at Worms. Compare the very functional *hôchgezît* at the gate with all the festivities at Worms. In addition, the speech in which the knights' wardrobe is dealt with (506) is parodistically reminiscent of the elaborate negotiations with Kriemhilde (343–371), particularly since on both occasions it is on Sifrid's recommendation that an attempt is being made to impress Brünnhilde.

488,1 ▪ The same introduction as at Worms (109,1).
See also note 482.

496,4 ▪ *zühte* is most naturally taken as genitive singular, referring to the same thing as 497,4. Sifrid is reluctant to let his treasurer feel the full force of his heavy hand. Compare his restraint towards Brünnhilde (459,1–2).
See also note 105,2.

500,1–3 ▪ This is precisely what Sifrid had wanted Gunther to prove when he first challenged him. It is also a denial of the distinction between *werc* and *gebaere* imposed on him at Isenstein (454,3) by his relationship with Gunther. (See notes 115,4; 454,3; 482).

The result of his victory over Alberich is that Sifrid steps back into his rightful place. He wins Nibelunge in order to keep it. Contrast the way he hands over all his winnings elsewhere (Liudegast, stanza 193; Brünnhilde; Brünnhilde's ring and girdle; the bear). The "handing-over" pattern suggests that he is in some way detached from the environment at these points; cf. Dietrich's handing over of Gunther and Hagen to Kriemhilde at the end (note 2353,1–3).

506 ■ See note 482.

511,4 ■ The question has been raised as to the precise way in which Brünnhilde singles out Sifrid from the rest. According to Bartsch (note to this line), she treats him with less deference than the others; according to Dürrenmatt[4] she treats him with more. But the important thing is that she cannot help reacting to Sifrid as if he were unique. She has already done it once, involuntarily (419). Now, following Gunther's advice, she does it again. This fits nicely into the triangle Gunther–Brünnhilde–Sifrid, in that Gunther consciously knows why Sifrid is outstanding, and why Brünnhilde should be polite to him. Brünnhilde's obedience on this occasion supplies the form to her own relationship with Sifrid, about which she knows nothing consciously.

514,2 ■ See note 55,4.

518,3 ■ See note 55,4.

521,4 ■ The brutal indifference of the Burgundians to any emotion that Brünnhilde might experience is made extraordinarily clear here. She has, after all, ruled very effectively on her own for some time; her riches are considerable, and her beauty is internationally renowned. Having surrendered all this, she is entitled to expect the winner to take some interest in the prize. Instead, he wants to leave as soon as possible, appoints a governor at her request in a decidedly off-hand manner, allows his underlings to jeer at her wealth, making it as clear as he can that her achievements up to now are expendable.

The Burgundian attitude seems all the more obnoxious, when one realises how little they have done to deserve the prize anyway. No wonder they are unable to appreciate it.

The haste of the Burgundians and Brünnhilde's rather bewildered reluctance are brought out when the following lines are compared: 474,4 with 475,1 (also 477,3–4); 512,4 with 513,1–3; 518,1–3 with 521,4; 522,1–2 with 522,3–4.

[4] N. Dürrenmatt, *Das Nibelungenlied im Kreise der höfischen Dichtung* (Diss., Bern, 1945), p. 50.

From line 523,4 emerges the pathetic hope that Gunther will come and help her rule, having proved his virility. The narrator knows better (526,4), since Gunther is doubly an imposter.

A parallel is afforded by Kriemhilde's later reluctance to leave Burgundy (691 ff.). In refusing her brother's offer of a dowry, Sifrid is much more considerate—perhaps because of his greater detachment.

523,4 ■ See note 343,4.

531,2 ■ The meaning of *kamere* is not immediately clear. Bartsch (note to this line) thought that Brünnhilde's treasure was meant, and de Boor (note to this line) chooses "Wohl und Verpflegung der Reisegesellschaft" from among the possibilities. The fact remains, however, that the word *kameraere* has just been used twice to mean treasurer (517,2; 518,4), and that both Hagen and Dankwart were at pains to show their expertise in this direction as against Brünnhilde's rather insignificant efforts. Whatever the precise nature of Hagen's proposed activities on the boat (and he gives no details, merely saying he makes a bad messenger), it is clear that he thinks of himself as the guardian of the Burgundians' fortune. This is an interesting anticipation of his later confiscation of the Nibelung treasure (perhaps because Kriemhilde is on the point of usurping his function?). There is also an element of re-assertion of rightful position, after his ignominious dependence on Sifrid as Isenstein (cf. also 1746,4, where he associates being *kameraere* with carrying his own weapons in defiance of Kriemhilde).

Sifrid is now reduced to his former status of the donkey who will carry anything provided that Kriemhilde is dangled in front of him (532,4; 535,2). The tasks so far allotted to him have been: unpaid mercenary, "horse," pimp, and now messenger. The prize all along has been Kriemhilde. From this angle it is not so surprising that the Burgundians should consider both Sifrid and Kriemhilde expendable when the time comes.

532,3–4 ■ See note 535,3.

535,3 ■ Gunther, as usual, prefers cliché to truth. Hagen had suggested Kriemhilde as the only effective "carrot" (532). Sifrid, not a tactful man, frankly justifies Hagen's feeling by ignoring the repeated: *nu leistet mînen muot* (534,1); *daz ich ez iemer diene* (534,2); *durch den willen mîn* (535,1), which lead up to the comfortable compromise formula of this line. Instead, he insists that he is doing it for Kriemhilde's sake alone (536,4). This recalls his earlier honesty on the way to Isenstein (388), and must be the cause of some irritation to Gunther, which he doubtless has no difficulty in repressing.

536,4 ■ See note 535,3.

538,4 ■ This is remarkable complacency, even for Gunther. It is equalled by the narrator (682,4), and repeated by Gunther just before he learns the unpleasant truth (632,2–3).
     See also note 659,4.

544,4 ■ For a discussion of *hôhiu minne* in this context, see note 47,1.

558,3–4 ■ This incident shows powerfully the discrepancy between Sifrid's real values and the ones he is trying to adopt. The *botenmiete* has a symbolic value for the court, and the giving of largesse also. Hagen especially takes it very seriously at Isenstein. But to Sifrid it is just an empty ritual which he is prepared to go through to please Kriemhilde. His returning of the money is a characteristically uncourtly (because naïve) excess of courtliness. He outdoes the court in its forms, but keeps showing that he sees no point in them. Compare his uncourtly generosity to the Danes and Saxons in the matter of money (315 and note; 691 ff.)
     Sifrid is just not acquisitive, whereas the court is. Trophies are an encumbrance to Sifrid and he leaves them lying around for someone else to fight over: Brünnhilde, his treasure, ring, girdle, even his wife.

563,1 ■ The common ending in -*olt* is a parodistic echo of the alliterating kings. For further evidence on the comic side of Rumold, see notes 343,4 and 1465 ff.

579–80 ▪ The sequence of events is not described very clearly, but it seems that Gunther and his company ride up to the bank of the Rhine opposite Worms, enter the ships and row hurriedly across, to be welcomed by Kriemhilde and her company on the bank near the city (580).

587–88 ▪ See note 771,3.

620,3 ▪ Compare 803,3. *eigenholde* occurs only twice in the *Nibelungenlied*, both times conveying Brünnhilde's conception of Sifrid's relationship to Gunther and herself. Its meaning in other works is nearer to "serf" than "vassal" (*man*), but this distinction is disregarded by Brünnhilde, as by Gunther. Within this work, *eigenholde* naturally suggests *eigen* and *holt*, especially if lines 1741,3 and 2372,3, with their parallel structure, are juxtaposed. *holt* describes a whole range of amicable relationships, including vassal (1466,2), lover-husband (2372,3) and well-disposed relative (919,3; 2134,4). *eigen* is used regularly of property and land (things one "owns," including the Nibelung treasure 526,1; 1741,3), then also of the dwarf Alberich's relationship to his conquerer (498,2), and lastly (chiefly by Brünnhilde) with unambiguous reference to Sifrid's and Kriemhilde's supposed vassalage (724,3; 830,1).

In the quarrel between the two queens, Brünnhilde claims Sifrid as her *eigen* (821,3; 827,2), and Kriemhilde sarcastically repeats the claim (*sît er dîn eigen ist* 825,1), in terms similar to her own later lament over the lost treasure: *der was doh mîn eigen* (1741,3). However we interpret the exact force of *eigen* in this exchange, it is fitting that Brünnhilde should express her claims on Sifrid by means of a word in which associations of bondship, ownership and love are difficult to separate.

See also note 821,3–4 and D. G. Mowatt, "Language, Literature and Middle High German," *Seminar*, I (1965), pp. 83–87. The reductive tendencies which mar Hugo Bekker's pleasantly relaxed discussions of central issues of the *Nibelungenlied* (*Germanic Review*, Vols. XLI–XLII, 1966–7) are most clearly seen in his limitation of the "Eigenmann"-motif to a counterpart of the kingship-motif. It is true that some interpretations are demonstrably "incorrect" (*Germanic Review*, Vol. XLII, pp. 13 f.), but it is illusory and repressive to suppose that a single correct one can be found, or that a relatively adequate one in terms of surface structure can rule out another one in terms of deep structure.

632,3 ■ See note 538,4.

633,1 ■ See note 343,4.

636,2–3 ■ Compare 677. The girdle stands for Gunther's impotence, as well as Brünnhilde's virginity.

638,3 ■ See note 55,4.

652,2 ■ Gunther never seems openly put out by Sifrid's recurrent tactlessness (694–5; 965–8).

655,4 ■ It would be a pity to treat this reaction of Gunther's as the fulfilment of some mediaeval norm, or to give it a dignity it conspicuously lacks. The gap between conventional assumption (*die mîne lieben frouwen*) and shocking reality (*ein vreislîchez wîp*) is characteristic of Gunther throughout his relationship with Brünnhilde. Compare the rhetoric of 329 and the clownish despair of 442 (notes 329 and 332–3).

659,4 ■ A most respectable line—as incongruous here as is line 682,4 after Sifrid's intervention, or 538,4 as a summary of Gunther's passive role in the bridal games at Isenstein (cf. note 538,4).

The incongruity undermines the formulaic force of the line (otherwise reminiscent of *Minnesang*), and reminds us of other possibilities in the word *minne* (see note 3,1). Gunther's real attitude to Brünnhilde is far from elevated. He wants her physically (stanza 625), and is prepared to have Sifrid usurp all but his most basic marital rights (stanza 655). If we add to this the fact that Sifrid has just dissipated all Gunther's husbandly concern by assuring him that he does not (or will not) "minnen" Brünnhilde, it is evident that Gunther's idea of *minne* is limited, earthy and acquisitive.

See also note 296.

670,2 ■ See note 416,1.

673 ■ This universality of Sifrid follows naturally from his super-human, mythological quality, and it is surprising that it finds so little echo elsewhere in the work. Perhaps it is because there are no real men for him to represent? The males in his vicinity want help, not an example to follow. Only Brünnhilde appreciates the significance of his exemplary acts, cf. stanza 678 and 461,2.

It seems to be generally accepted in the *Nibelungenlied* that women have to be kept in order (Hagen 1130,1–2; Sifrid 862), and conversely, that it is dishonourable to be outmatched by a woman (Dankwart 443,4; Hildebrand 2374,2). The fact remains that no one in the poem except Sifrid (and, in a way, Hildebrand) ever translates this into effective action.

678,1 ■ The *du* form here seems to be submissive and personal in contrast to the cold, official *ir* of 635,1. *du* and *ir* are not always distinguished to such good effect in the *Nibelungenlied*, careless-ness and the requirements of rhyme certainly playing a part (162,2). But usage normally only fluctuates when the characters concerned are of more or less equal standing and enjoy a many-sided relationship (cf. 339–42, 390–93); and frequently the fluc-tuation has a point (cf. Sifrid's familiarity 453–55, Brünnhilde's attempt at dignity 846, and 356,1 note). The *du* in 1440,2–3 may be considered either an archaic ceremonial *du* (cf. "thou"), or an attempt by a junior ambassador to give himself the dignity of his master (contrast 1193).

Gustav Ehrismann's article on the subject[5] is one of the few early studies to illuminate the actual text.

680,2 ■ The narrator's query invites the reader to speculate on why Sifrid takes Brünnhilde's girdle and ring. Clearly he is in a sense entitled to them, since he is essentially responsible for her loss of maidenhood; equally clearly he need not have taken them, since he left her to Gunther to deflower. Similarly, he need not have handed them over to Kriemhilde (684,2), though this action

[5] *Zeitschrift für deutsche Wortforschung*, Vol. IV (1903), pp. 210 ff.

too is appropriate, since it was to win Kriemhilde that Sifrid mastered Brünnhilde.

The suggestion of arrogance, thoughtlessness for others, and careless superiority contained in *hôhen muot* (680,2) is a permanent feature of Sifrid's behaviour. His inhuman generosity and lack of acquisitiveness belong here too.[6]

See also note 558,3–4.

682,4 ◾ Ironic lines of this nature are common in the *Nibelungenlied*; superficially true, their essential falsity stresses the difference between appearance and reality, and illuminates both the characters in the work and their codes of behaviour. This line immediately recalls Gunther's own fatuous boast (538,4): *dar nâch ie ranc mîn herze, wie wol ich daz verendet hân!* With double irony, the first part of this latter is merely a repetition of Sifrid's ironic words (393,3) when helping Gunther to identify Brünnhilde among the Isenstein maidens. The two layers of Gunther's ignominy are thus bracketed together, and it is impossible to read any of these three lines without being made aware of the actual events which make them hollow. Gunther's main survival trait is his ability to live in the present, and on the surface; but his words continually revive the past, and uncover the mess underneath.

See also note 659,4.

691 ff. ◾ Compare stanzas 519 ff., where a similar situation arises at Isenstein. The comparison is in Sifrid's favour: indulgence, polite indifference (694–5), as against jeering and insensitive boastfulness (519; 521,4). See also note 711,1–3. Kriemhilde suffers similarly by comparison with Brünnhilde. Instead of justified pride in her own achievement, she shows a rather childish insistence on getting her fair share out of her brothers (especially in

---

[6] J. K. Bostock, "The Message of the *Nibelungenlied*," *Modern Language Review* (1960), p. 203, notes some of these characteristics of Sifrid, but is led into a blind alley by his assumption that the poet is consciously holding Sifrid up as an object-lesson to young courtly gentlemen of the time. This assumption also stands in the way of an adequate statement about Sifrid's relationship with Brünnhilde. Bostock's suggestion (p. 205) that Sifrid "dislikes" Brünnhilde's "type" is not very satisfying.

stanza 696), and an irresponsibility about the unity of Burgundy which foreshadows her later destructiveness. It is difficult to avoid the impression, here and elsewhere, that Sifrid and Brünnhilde are grown up in some sense that the Burgundians are not. One only has to think of their earlier fussing over clothes (350 ff.) and protocol (355–6), or their later jealous squabbles over the treasure, and of Hagen's intense irritation when chosen as part of Kriemhilde's share (stanza 698). Does she suggest it just to annoy him? See also note 774.

698,2 ■ See note 343,4.

709,1. ■ Here, as in Hartmann,[7] *lachen* is evidence of confident and relaxed security, often associated with *vester muot* (e.g. *Der arme Heinrich* 1136; *Erec* 8118), rather than of uproarious amusement. The opposition appears most clearly in *Der arme Heinrich* (1107–10; 1003–7), where *lachen* goes with the certainty of death, and *weinen* with *zwîfel*. In the *Nibelungenlied*, as Wachinger has shown, the whole courtly scene from time to time unfolded is set against a background of impending disaster. The continual emphasis on *hôher muot, fröide, lachen*, thus builds up tension as well as tedium.

The two occurrences of (*er*)*smielen* (447,2; 728,3), which also expresses amusement, are both used to describe the attitude of someone who knows more than his interlocuter. In the case of Brünnhilde (447,2), one may assume a feeling of superiority, even contempt. In the case of Gunther (728,3), the extra knowledge can only have lessened his confidence, and his smile must have been wry, or at least ironic.

It is likely that both *lachen* and (*er*)*smielen* refer to smiling rather than laughing. They are, however, far from being synonyms.

711,1–3 ■ After the striking difference between Worms and Santen in the matter of receptions and levies (see also note 482), it comes as no surprise that the ceremonies at Sifrid's court are in

[7] *Iwein* 391; 855; 6279; 7303. *Der arme Heinrich* 1107–10; 968; 1003–7. *Erec* 8028; 8119; 8153–7.

fact more lavish than the much lauded feast at Worms. It also seems appropriate to Sifrid's ambience that the fact is stated simply; and that after one stanza of description (712), the symbolic largesse of Sigelinde is followed up by Sigemund's very practical gift of kingship.

The objective fact that Sifrid is richer than Gunther (695,3) is again apparent when the two queens quarrel. Kriemhilde's women are quite simply better dressed than Brünnhilde's (836).

714 ■ We usually assume that there is something exemplary about Sifrid's behaviour as king, but if so, it is a very different standard from the one embodied in Gunther. Sifrid is characteristically associated with real power and real strength (cf. 723,4). We are not surprised to read here that his subjects feared him, especially when we remember the everyday treatment meted out to Alberich and the gate-keeper.

With a personal objective, signifying a permanent relationship, *vürhten* is used twice of Sifrid and his subjects (714,4; 723,4), once of Etzel and his subjects (1429,3), and never of Gunther and his. Other uses are as follows: Sigelinde fears the Burgundians (60,3); the Saxon messengers fear Gunther (142,4—but see the note on this line); Brünnhilde's ladies fear Dankwart (414,4), and Brünnhilde—with some relish—fears Sifrid (416,4).

See also note 43,3–4.

715,2 ■ Time in the *Nibelungenlied* does not correspond in many respects to time as experienced in real life: thus, for instance, nobody ages noticeably in the work.

This issue is discussed more fully in Burghart Wachinger's *Studien zum Nibelungenlied: Vorausdeutungen, Aufbau, Motivierung* (Tübingen, 1960), p. 83. He also makes the point (p. 129) that the cumulative effect of all the time that elapses does have a function in the work, in that Kriemhilde can eventually be criticized as *lancraeche* (1461,4).

One unmistakeable feature of the way time is used in the poem is to structure the plot in a very simple way. The major time intervals break up the plot into an alternating series of states of rest and of sequences of action, each action sequence being initiated

by a single person and coming to an end when this person has achieved his objective (regardless of who or what else is involved):
Initial state of rest.
Sifrid woos and wins Kriemhilde.
Ten years pass.
Brünnhilde investigates and disposes of Sifrid.
Thirteen years pass.
Etzel woos and wins Kriemhilde.
Thirteen years pass.
Kriemhilde seeks and obtains revenge.
Final state of rest.
Note that within the first action sequence (Sifrid's courtship) there occurs a subordinate pause of one year, broken by the Saxon initiative—and then by that of Gunther.
See also note 138,3.

716–718 ▪ It is characteristic of the two marriages that Kriemhilde should bear a Gunther, and Brünnhilde a Sifrid. The two reasons for choosing names are nicely distinguished. Kriemhilde, thinking of her family and its traditions, hopes that her son will grow up like his uncle—a forlorn hope with such a father. Brünnhilde merely makes the gesture *durch des heldes liebe*—there is no question of a second Sifrid. It is also made clear that Gunther himself, relying more on environment than on blood, is determined to bring his son up as a useful member of society (*biderbe* 719,3). The word is applied to soldiers as well, and in a soldierly context its meaning is close to "brave," but only because a "good" soldier is the same as a "brave" soldier. In a wider social context, its meaning must be wider. As it happens, the society at Worms values bravery, among other things, but not of the superhuman Sifrid-like variety. By making his son *biderbe*, Gunther is training him to follow the ideals of Burgundy, and only to emulate Sifrid in so far as Sifrid is a good Burgundian (cf. 818,2; 935,1; 1193,1; 1347,3; 2134,3).

723,4 ▪ See note 714.

724,3–4 ▪ Except in one respect, the whole sequence of interrelated events set in motion by Sifrid's decision to woo Kriemhilde has come to a satisfactory conclusion (emphasized by the idyllic naming of the two sons after their father's best friends, for which see also note 716–18); only Brünnhilde is not utterly content— because one condition of her acceptance of Gunther's suit, namely that Sifrid is Gunther's vassal (423,1), does not seem to be ful- filled.

This is the legal, rationalized side of her uneasiness. Its more immediate cause is stated in line 2. Brünnhilde cannot stand Kriemhilde's pretensions (cf. 730; 618–22), and insists on proving that Gunther is really better than Sifrid. This is what their quarrel is about (see note 815,3–4). In the event, Brünnhilde uncovers the opposite, less palatable truth, hinted at in stanzas 695 and 720–3, and most clearly expressed in 836, that Sifrid is richer, as well as stronger than Gunther.

See also notes 711,1–3; 725,2–3; 730.

725,2–3 ▪ Brünnhilde's conscious worries are restricted to the feudal relationships; and in this sense, *dienen* helps to specify the sense of *eigen* (724,3). The fact remains that *vremde* and *dienen* generally (cf. MF passim), and *eigen* in the *Nibelungenlied* (see note 620,3), are saturated with erotic connotations; it would be an act of misdirected puritanism to rule these out. Once it is accepted that Brünnhilde's motives for re-establishing contact with Sifrid are complex, the way is open to a larger understanding of the quarrel between the two queens. Hagen's reasons for killing Sifrid also appear more confused, and more interesting.

See also notes 724,3–4; 870.

728,3 ▪ See note 709,1.

730 ▪ There can be no doubt from this stanza, and especially the last line, that Brünnhilde is comparing herself with Kriemhilde as a fit object for Sifrid's love. The occasion to which she explicitly refers (730,3) was passed over by the narrator with the remark that "Brünnhilde wept" (618,3).

Apart from these concealed motives, her treatment of Gunther is masterly. By assuming he has unlimited power over Sifrid, she makes the whole matter seem like a trifling favour which would nevertheless mean a lot to his little wife. This technique, indicative of a "new" Brünnhilde, is predictably successful at Worms. It produces in 731 a testy acceptance from her husband, in which he makes some show of living up to the mightiness she lays on him: "of course it is a simple matter. I shall send messengers, and they will come." She immediately follows this (732) by tying him down to more definite arrangements. She demands to know (1) when the messengers will be sent, (2) when the guests will be required to appear, and (3) the names of the messengers. Gunther understands the position, and calls in the messengers on the spot (733). The actual message which he gives them is humble in the extreme, with its emphasis on *holder* (734,4), *dienende* (735,2), *im vil êren gan* (735,4) and *waege* (736,2). Gunther at least is in no doubt of the favour Sifrid will be conferring on him if he comes, and he is concerned that Sifrid should take it in the same way (734,2).

See also note 748,1–2.

739,2 ▣ From Niderlant, to which Sifrid returns with Kriemhilde (708), via a mention of Sifrid's twofold possessions (720–21), the scene of his activities shifts to the land of Nibelunge. Furthermore it is to this latter that Kriemhilde thinks of returning after Sifrid's death (1085,3), though it is to Niderlant that her father-in-law in fact retires (1098,3). Kriemhilde's thoughts might be explained by the later revelation that she was given the treasure as a wedding present (1116,4); but a clear rational relationship between the two disparate territories of Sifrid is no more to be expected than between the two disparate aspects of his character.

On the other hand, it is natural that Kriemhilde should be preoccupied with the *Nibelunge* aspect, since it includes the source of Sifrid's power, which stays with her and Hagen (treasure; sword; Nibelungs—see note 1526,2). Her lack of interest in the *Niderlant* aspect, which includes all that is progressive and mature in her marriage, is paralleled by her attitude to her court at Etzelnburg. A striking common feature is her repeated rejection of motherhood. Could it be that her warning dream and her decision to remain untouched (see notes 13,2; 17,2–4) arose more out of fear of parturition than out of modesty? See also notes 87,4 and 1526, 2.

748,1–2 ◼ Sifrid dismisses the elaborate formulae which Gunther has thought out. You just trust friends, and that's the end of it. He also assumes that Gunther's protestations are only a cover for some new request for help (749). He, at least, is in no doubt as to the true relationship between himself and Gunther (cf. 728,3–4). Cf. also stanza 759,2–4, where his willingness to help in suitable ways is contrasted with his impatience at a relatively pointless request.
See also notes 55,4; 730.

755–6 ◼ The formalities at Santen are more functional than those at Worms: from Gunther, elaborate politeness, based on doubt and deceit; from Sifrid and Sigemund, a friendly and honest immediacy. Gunther's invitation (734–7) was dragged from him in order to hide from Brünnhilde the real reasons why he would rather Sifrid kept his distance. Sifrid's reaction (748–9) shows his unquestioning acceptance of the real relationship, and Sigemund's own invitation (755), given in the name of friendship, is a startling contrast to Gunther's devious reluctance.
See also notes 482; 771,3.

759,2–4 ◼ See note 748,1–2.

771,3 ◼ In his note to this line, de Boor has pointed out that Gere does not answer Brünnhilde's question, and that Uote's question is contrasted with Brünnhilde's, but he has failed to follow up an interesting line of enquiry: Brünnhilde's concentration on Kriemhilde's *zuht* is also noticeable in 730,1 and is stated there to derive from their first meeting—on which occasion Kriemhilde's *zuht* is mentioned three times in five lines (587,1 ff.). Furthermore, the sense of strain and formality in Kriemhilde's reception of Brünnhilde is contrasted with the warmth and pleasure of Sigelinde's greeting to Kriemhilde herself a little later (stanza 709). There, *durch zühte* is replaced by *mit lachendem munde* and *durch liebe*.

As we might expect, relationships in general are both warmer and less controlled in Santen than in Worms.
See also notes 346; 755–6.

774 ■ There is a note of envy and irritation in the first line of this stanza, which reflects not only on Sifrid's vast wealth, but also on his negligent attitude towards it. Wealth and generosity are much more serious problems for the Burgundians.
See also notes 691 ff.; 711,1–3.

777 ■ See note 343,4.

783,2–3 ■ As well as a natural desire to stop Brünnhilde from being rude to his powerful guest, Gunther shows a characteristic obsession with external form. He fusses (782,4). Brünnhilde's answer refers him back to reality, just as Sifrid's had the Burgundian messengers (748–9).

788,3 ■ The ability to be *ungefüege* is one of Sifrid's outstanding characteristics (190,3; 670,3). Brünnhilde had it too, before being subdued (440,3; 676,1). In a public situation, as here, it extends to Sifrid's whole company (cf. 800), so that the approach of this savage cloud of dust must have produced in Brünnhilde an echo of her earlier reaction when Sifrid, alone, had approached her virginal bed. At all events, the same word *ungefüege* is used on both occasions. Bartsch (in his *Wörterbuch* to the *Nibelungenlied*) glosses it variously as: (1) "übermässig gross und stark," (2) "unschicklich, grob," (3) "gewaltig, schlimm," and (4) "unfügsam wild." Translation naturally varies with the context, but there are no occurrences in the poem where the basic meaning of "socially unacceptable" is ruled out completely.

802,3–803,3 ■ These lines show the impossibility of Gunther's hopes. Sifrid's "old position" was that of a knight without followers, eager helper, candidate for Kriemhilde's favours. By now, as Brünnhilde must eventually realize in spite of all Gunther's efforts, he has a wife and kingdom of his own. Hence this unruly and obtrusive crowd of knights that always needs accommodating, as well as Sifrid.

See also notes 788,3 and 1526,2.

804,2 ■ The spilled wine makes a sudden entry and exit, and is usually dismissed as a loose end left by the author, possibly from an earlier version. It does have echoes however, in two other places where drinking becomes an obtrusive activity: the hunt scene and the blood-drinking scene, near the end. In the hunt scene, Sifrid complains extravagantly that he was not given his fill of wine to drink (965–70). His irritation recalls his reaction to the news that they only needed him for a trivial hunting expedition, and not for war (909; cf: note 194). If these outbursts, and the bear escapade, are both in some way reactions to a frustrated fighting instinct, then the equation "fill of wine=fill of blood" is only just under the surface. This would add point to Sifrid's imminent murder, and prepare for the later scene where the equation is inverted, with macabre jocularity, by Hagen (2114–16).

Against this background, the present incident recalls all the blood yet to be spilt. The pointless extravagance and wastage also contrast with the two later scenes, where the need is desperate and the wine missing (970,1; 2114,2). Burgundian wine, it suggests, is plentiful, except when people are thirsty.

814,3 ■ *durch kurzewîle wân.* The phrase strengthens the impression, gradually built up throughout the long-drawn-out ceremonials at Worms, that the narrator does not whole-heartedly embrace this way of life as an absolute ideal. Compare the Worms-Santen contrasts mentioned before.

See also notes 482; 755–6.

815,3–4 ■ It is at first sight surprising that Kriemhilde should be the one to raise the question of Sifrid's position so provocatively. But perhaps Brünnhilde, being more aware of her worries on this score, has herself in better control? Kriemhilde, like Brünnhilde, apparently feels the need for the relationship between Sifrid and the Burgundians to be clarified. As Brünnhilde can only accept having married into the Burgundian world provided Sifrid is part

of it, so Kriemhilde can only accept her marriage to Sifrid provided her kinsmen acknowledge her husband's superiority. From
this point of view it does not much matter who speaks first (see
also notes 724,3–4; 817).

His "courtship" of Kriemhilde makes Sifrid temporarily more
courtly (123,4); has Kriemhilde's marriage made her permanently
more boastful, like Sifrid? She certainly echoes his original challenge (110,3–4), made before he undertook to accommodate himself to Burgundy.

816,2–3 ■ These two lines express the central inadequacy of
Sifrid, and it is fitting that it should be stated by the dispossessed
Brünnhilde. Sifrid does indeed need the world to himself (with
mate) in order to be fully realized. The attempt to merge his absolute individuality with Kriemhilde's social dependence leads to his
destruction. Brünnhilde understands, far better than Kriemhilde
(cf. stanza 904), that Sifrid's surpassing excellence is an essential
part of his inability to fit into society. Hence the apparent irrelevance of this immediate reaction of hers to Kriemhilde's opening
statement (stanza 815). She does not dispute Sifrid's title to the
extravagant praise offered by Kriemhilde, she only questions
Kriemhilde's right to offer it; and she does this by putting the
praise firmly back where she and Sifrid belong. Kriemhilde makes
no answer to this (stanzas 817; 819), but continues to praise her
husband until she realizes (stanza 822) the status implication of
what Brünnhilde is saying (821,3).

817 ■ Kriemhilde's appeal is to the visible (lines 1–3) fact of
Sifrid's pre-eminence. On this score, she is far more confident (line
4) than Brünnhilde, who has no tangible proof that her choice was
the right one. On the other hand, Sifrid's real excellence is not
universally and publicly acknowledged, whereas Gunther's supposed worth is. This is what undermines Kriemhilde's security,
and drives her to her opening provocative statement (815,3–4).
Since she knows, or thinks she knows, that she has not had Sifrid
entirely to herself (stanza 840), it is in her interest to believe that
Sifrid is larger than life.

820,3–4 ■ So far the ladies have kept their spite under control, a control reflected in the way each little speech ends with the end of the stanza. Now Brünnhilde's long suppressed complaint bursts this bond and flows over into the following stanza. In her emotion she does not distinguish between the two separate but related occasions on which Gunther won her: in the tournament and in the bedroom. They are, in any case, only stages in the same process.

See also note 459–461.

821,3–4 ■ The force of *übele geschehen* (line 4) depends on the meaning given to *eigen* (line 3). If this is limited to the social status implied, then Kriemhilde's complaint is indeed mediaeval, and concerned with status above all else. But if *eigen* is allowed to imply possession in a more general way, both Brünnhilde's claim and Kriemhilde's reaction would refer to the intimate and intricate triangular relationship which holds them together (see also note 620,3).

It is also true that Kriemhilde's power does depend quite literally on Sifrid's position (as it does later on that of Etzel). Unlike Brünnhilde, she was never queen in her own right; she is correspondingly extreme in her ambition (cf. 829,2–3). This argument is thus a struggle for absolute power between Kriemhilde and Brünnhilde, fought out over their rivalry for possession of Sifrid.

See also note 825,1–4.

822,2 ■ *wine* is not uncommon in various situations in the *Nibelungenlied*. Editors usually gloss it as a word of archaic flavour, with connotations of pre-courtly, less formalized sexual relationship. In a public, very courtly situation such as the present one, it could be considered as an insult. The fact remains that there are two occurrences in the work where the situation is public, and the word clearly not slighting. In 554,1, Sifrid describes Brünnhilde as Gunther's *wine* (="bride"?), while addressing Kriemhilde. Admittedly the word is not entirely appropriate to Gunther's real situation, but no one takes offence. In 2135,2, the narrator refers to Rüdeger as Gotelinde's *wine*.

If Kriemhilde can think of it as an insult in this context, it shows how little importance she is attaching to the relationship itself, and how much to the status deriving from it. The real slight is of course in the whole phrase *eigen mannes wine*.

Similar ambiguities occur 622,4.

825,1–4 ■ Once the physical possession implied in *eigen* (821,3; 827,2) is accepted, this sneer of Kriemhilde's becomes more venomous than ever. It also adds barb to her later revelation (840). Not only can she disclose that *her* husband first enjoyed Brünnhilde; she can also boast that he left her for metal more attractive. Poor Brünnhilde is thus demoted (by owning an inferior husband), dishonoured, and discarded. The same ambiguity was apparent in *dienen* (see note 725,2–3).

See also note 620,3.

827,2 ■ See notes 725,2–3; 825,1–4.

827,4 ■ For Kriemhilde to enter the church before Brünnhilde does not prove her claim justified; it simply makes the claim public and challenges Brünnhilde to contest it publicly. In the event, psychological considerations alone determine which lady enters the church first: Kriemhilde confounds Brünnhilde by an unexpected counter-attack. But see also note 711,1–3.

829,2–3 ■ Kriemhilde's intention to outshine all queens that have ever been exceeds the relevant one of outshining Brünnhilde—and reveals a hitherto concealed aspect of her character. Once revealed, it throws much light on her strange action of marrying Sifrid, and also on Hagen's determination to cut her down to size.

See also notes 356,1 and 691 ff.

836 ■ See notes 711,1–3 and 724,3–4.

839,1 ■ The unemotional aside (*zornec was ir muot*) is a particularly nice example of the narrator's customary detachment.

841,2 ■ Kriemhilde's mocking of Brünnhilde for allegedly permitting (or ordering?)[8] Sifrid to deflower her does not necessarily

---

[8] The word *lieze* is not, in itself, specific on this point (cf. 315,4).

imply that Brünnhilde permitted this knowingly. It does, however, suggest that she was a fool not to know and recognize it. In
any case, Kriemhilde does not really accept Brünnhilde's claim to
ownership of herself and Sifrid. By hammering home the *list* (line
1) and *lieze* (line 2), she is also laying bare the barrenness of
Brünnhilde's pretensions. If Sifrid really were Brünnhilde's *eigen*,
then she must have ordered him to bed with her, such being the
nature of feudal relationships. The terminology follows naturally
from the relationship claimed. Since the claim is ridiculous, the
act is also ridiculed. On top of all this, Kriemhilde also manages to
suggest (perhaps for her own peace of mind?) that Brünnhilde
could only get Sifrid into bed with her by pulling her rank on
him.[9]

853,4 ■ Gunther's native caution seldom deserts him. His answer
is a masterpiece of compression, and leaves him committed to no
belief and no action: "If what you say is true (*so*), then Kriemhilde would have been (*hete*) acting wrongly." He shows little
trust in Brünnhilde, and no indignation at her discomfiture. The
question of Kriemhilde's reliability is carefully left open (855,2;
857,2), so that Sifrid can deny everything. In the event, Sifrid
refuses to co-operate in Gunther's face-saving procedures; he
promises to thrash Kriemhilde, and denies having told her anything (858), but he cannot be bothered to deny her actual revelation.

860,1 ■ Possibly this line implies that Sifrid actually takes the
oath, not merely that he prepares to do so and is interrupted by
Gunther. (The distinction is not very important; see Wachinger,
Studien (1960), p. 112 and footnote 4.)
   Gunther's promise to take no action (*ledic lân*, line 3) goes back
to his undertaking in 859,3, where it was made conditional on
Sifrid's swearing of the oath (859,2). The oath in question, suggested by Sifrid, was that of 858,4, namely, that he had *said* nothing to Kriemhilde. Sifrid raises his hand to swear this in 860,1,

---

[9] Werner Schröder, "Die Tragödie Kriemhilts im *Nibelungenlied*," *Zeitschrift
für deutsches Altertum*, Vol. XC (1960–61), p. 72, also reacts to Kriemhilde's
insecurity here, but interprets it in more dignified, less personal terms.

and the simplest reason for Gunther's hurried exculpation is that Sifrid has omitted denying the actual misdemeanour. (There is after all always the risk that, if further pressed, Sifrid might come out with the truth.) So Gunther accepts the offered oath as second best, and himself establishes Sifrid's innocence of the more serious charge (860,4).

Sifrid and Gunther are also the people to whom the last line of stanza 861 refers most naturally (but see also note 861,4). They have just collaborated in hushing up an unpleasant truth, known only to themselves, and might well exchange glances. They are also caught in a posture which shows off the stock epithets *guot* and *gemeit* at their most hollow, but the irony here is truly "dramatic," in the sense that the hollowness is apparent only to the narrator and his audience. The characters themselves seem to believe that their reputations are preserved, and Hagen has to work hard to whip up feeling against Sifrid. One of his accusations even turns out to be the one thing that Sifrid took the trouble to deny (867,3).

861,4 ■ This line has been taken as describing a reaction to Gunther's hasty dismissal of the case. The narrator's choice of position, however, is in the middle of a tactless disclosure on the part of Sifrid. It may well have come as a shock in such a courtly context to hear Sifrid complacently threatening his wife and advising the king to do the same. But the narrator does not tell us who was shocked, or whether they felt dismay, or liberation, or ironic recognition of something they had long suspected in Sifrid. At all events, such a reaction, on anyone's part, would suggest that Sifrid's apology is at least as *ungefüege* as his wife's behaviour. But see also note 860,1.

863,4 ■ Hagen's relegation (see note 119,3) is at its most extreme here, and so is his antagonism to Sifrid. On other occasions, before and after, he appears as sufficiently independent not to attend automatically on Gunther, but then he is sent for when a crisis threatens (stanzas 81–82 and 1177). And in general whatever Sifrid has done for the Burgundians has been on Hagen's advice (stanzas 151 and 331). Sifrid has, however, long since escaped

Hagen's net, and his relationship to Gunther and Brünnhilde has
a personal aspect. So his actions have consequences of their own,
and Hagen is not called in to deal with them. It is at this stage that
he strikes Sifrid down.

See also note 993.

864 ▪ Brünnhilde's humiliation arises from a combination of
factors of the greatest complexity; no totally satisfactory solution
is possible—at least not without a full confession by Gunther. In
this dilemma Gunther is prepared to tolerate his wife's tears and
the discontent of his men (871,4), but Hagen is not. He imposes a
quite different solution: by repudiating all bonds of friendship
and kinship with both Sifrid and Kriemhilde, by murdering Sifrid
and openly harassing his widow, Hagen seeks to establish that
these two were solely responsible for the scandal which touched
the court. True honour is thus sacrificed to reputation—hence the
many references to the *untriuwe* of the deed—but at least Brünnhilde can hold her head high once again (1100,1).

867,1 ▪ See note 870.

868 ▪ Gunther is, of course, in the best possible position to know
exactly how loyal and willing Sifrid has been. Still, he does admit
it handsomely and openly, and we see how his contact with Sifrid
can lift the curtain of courtly ceremonial for an instant, while he
recognizes a sort of service which is unforced and unregulated,
and based on human relationship instead of the more usual self-
interest. The curtain quickly falls back, however, and his later
behaviour seems even less excusable after his one glimpse of something better.

870 ▪ The suggestion that Gunther would acquire more lands
by killing Sifrid is as vague and irrelevant as the suggestion that
otherwise bastards will be reared at Worms (867,1). Hagen is
using any arguments he can to get his way.

The irrelevance is, however, only on the conscious level. The
two underlying suggestions, namely, that Sifrid is potentially a
greater king and a more virile lover than Gunther, are excellent

reasons for killing him. The argument about *gouche* is perhaps best resolved by taking it as literally as possible: "are we to be nursemaids to Sifrid's leavings?", or: "do we have to put up with this cuckoo in our midst until he takes over completely?" The associations of cuckoos gradually becoming too big to handle are particularly appropriate to Sifrid's position at Worms. The naming of the children might well have added to Hagen's uneasiness (see note 716–718).

872 ■ The confusion and weakness of Gunther are nowhere better seen than in the contrasting reasons he gives for not killing Sifrid: it would be immoral—and dangerous! From here on the three kings have twinges of conscience in following Hagen in his single-minded hostility to Sifrid and Kriemhilde; but they follow him all the same—at least until Etzel's intervention seems to offer them an alternative. Their present slight reluctance to benefit from Hagen's crime later gives them the illusion of innocence (1209; 1213; 1460–3). It also makes their fate inevitable, by rendering them deaf to Hagen's warnings.
    See also notes 1078,3; 1204,1–3; 1206,3; 1459,1.

873,2 ■ See note 55,4.

880,4 ■ When it is only a question of play-acting, Gunther can put on a show of anger. Contrast his previous reaction to a genuine threat (note 142,4).

884,4 ■ See note 343,4.

886,1 ■ This is the second time Sifrid has suggested that Gunther's place is in the home (see 174,1), and this time he proposes to dispense with Gunther's followers too. Whatever Gunther's original feelings were to such protectiveness, there is no doubt now what he thinks (887,1–3). Parodistically, Gunther repeats this assessment of himself when in extremity as Isenstein (442,3–4).

893,4 ■ Kriemhilde remembers that Hagen may possibly be Sifrid's enemy at the very moment of informing him of Sifrid's only weakness—but does not connect the two points until it is too late, first in a dream, then consciously (920 f.).

See also note 1010,4; and above p. 15.

896,3 ■ See above, p. 15.

898,1–2 ■ Kriemhilde's divided loyalty is in her mind at the moment of betrayal. She is a true Burgundian to think Sifrid needs Hagen to protect him in battle, and when he murders him instead, she still feels more at home with the murderers than with the bereaved (1081; 1085; 1088). Perhaps this is why she cannot rest until all her family are finally destroyed.

See also note 1082,1.

909 ■ Sifrid's anger, here and in stanzas 965–8, needs comment. Thematically, the hunt scene is parallel to the Isenstein expedition but at one extra remove from reality and satisfaction. Sifrid's relationship with Worms is largely one of frustration, and it comes in two waves:

(1) *First arrival—marriage—withdrawal*
 (a) Challenge to Gunther
 (b) Burgundian reaction—request for help:
   (i) Saxon war (virility harnessed with clear objective)
   (ii) Competitive games (Isenstein expedition) with Nibelung escapade
 (c) Reward—Kriemhilde

(2) *Second arrival—betrayal—death*
 (a) Danger to Gunther (unwitting provocation—quarrel of queens)
 (b–1) Burgundian reaction—dishonest request for help:
   (i) Saxon war, which never materializes
 (b–2) Further Burgundian reaction—invitation to compete and excel, as substitute for help in Saxon war:
   (i) Hunt (virility as an end in itself)
   (ii) Competitive games (race to well) with bear escapade
 (c) Reward—death.

There is nothing rigid or one-dimensional about this parallelism, and other alignments would be possible; but the extra degree of frustration, unreality and pointlessness makes sense of Sifrid's irritation (a side of him which appears now for the first time). From the Burgundian point of view, Sifrid might be said to go one step further towards intolerability in this scene. His excellence and self-reliance in the hunt are if anything more obtrusive than his single-handed conduct of the Saxon war—perhaps because his achievements are now in open competition with the Burgundians (but see also note 886,1). In the race for the well (parallel to the Isenstein games), he repeats his earlier pattern of first winning, and then handing over the prize to Gunther. But he then goes on to drink from the well himself, thus enacting Kriemhilde's accusation of cuckoldry.

The bear episode is formally parallel to the Nibelung jaunt, in that both are lapses into natural behaviour by a Sifrid who is almost submerged in pointlessness and deceit. In one sense, the bear is Brünnhilde, caught by Sifrid, set loose in Burgundian society, captured a second time by Sifrid, and finally rendered harmless. But whereas Brünnhilde was spared penetration and death (see note 459–461), the bear is less gently treated. In another sense, the bear is Sifrid himself, an uncomfortable guest in Burgundian society, a well-meaning disaster (the bear is only trying to run away), and finally a ritual murder victim. And in so far as Sifrid and Brünnhilde are one composite symbol, the bear is the spark in their relationship that Sifrid stamped out.

See also note 804,2.

912,3–4 ■ Compare 174,3 (belîbet bî den frouwen) and 886,1 (hie heime bestân), where Gunther himself is benevolently left at home by Sifrid. The seriousness and reality of the situations in which Gunther's presence is not required are in startling contrast to the present unsavoury charade, of which he is the central figure. In addition, the word hövschen recalls its only other occurrence in the work (350,3), where Gunther, again as central figure with Sifrid helping, originally went courting.

913,1 ■ Compare 917,1, where the same word hêrlîch ("proud,"

"haughty," "arrogant") is again used. It is as if Sifrid's social
sense grows weaker as his death approaches. Compare further his
supernatural demands in 968, and his denial of the social side of
a hunting party (913,3–4; 932).

916,4 ▪ The last half-line is ironic: literally true (in theory) with
reference to hunting wild animals, essentially false with reference
to murdering Sifrid. Compare 989,1 and 1002,2. It is also literally false (in fact), when seen in the context of Sifrid's outstanding bravery both in battle and in the hunt, where the Burgundians
are outclassed with contemptuous ease, especially in the matter of
capturing bears single-handed (957 ff.).

917,3–4 ▪ Here and at 1010,4 the poet emphasizes Brünnhilde's
part in urging Sifrid's death more than he does elsewhere. It is
unnecessary, however, to assume a mistake (there is no actual
contradiction, cf. 845,4 and 863 ff.), especially since such small
inconsequences are a regular feature of the poet's style. (Cf. the
introduction of Alberich, 336,3, without reference to his previous
naming, 96,2; the failure to explain how the cross sewn on Sifrid's
fighting apparel—and carefully noted by Hagen, 908,1—seems to
reappear on his hunting clothes, 980,4; cf. also the embarrassed
account of how Dankwart learns of Kriemhilde's promise to
Bloedelin, 1928,3). Here, as elsewhere, the mediaeval author
shows a great sensitivity to meaningful relationships and a casual
disregard of orderliness for its own sake (see above, pp. 9–16).
    The symbolism of 917,3 underlines Brünnhilde's connection
with Sifrid's death, both as instigator, and as innocent cause.
Compare 970,3; 976,4; 977,4.
    See also notes 909; 980,1; 1477.

923,4 ▪ Sifrid shows little insight here, but his behaviour is consistent. He merely repeats the official cliché, which he makes the
mistake of believing. It is a natural mistake, based on ignorance.
For if Kriemhilde had not just given him away to Hagen, there
would be no need for him to look beneath the surface. As it is,
Kriemhilde has undermined his invulnerability, and is naturally

plagued by omens, but still seems unable to give him any specific or useful warning.

932 ■ This independence recalls the lone Sifrid who left Santen for Worms (59,1).
See also notes 909; 913,1.

935,4 ■ The terrible lion on the Rhine helps to make Sifrid's behaviour unquestionably superhuman. The list of animals in stanza 937 is particularly impressive, and recalls his equally incredible feats in the Saxon war. Compare Hagen's moment of complete incredibility when he ferries the Burgundians single-handed across the Danube. See note 1572,3–4.

946,4 ■ For an interesting interpretation of the bear episode, see W. J. Schröder, "Das Nibelungenlied. Versuch einer Deutung" (1954–5).
See also note 909, which contains an analysis different in many respects from Schröder's.

965–8 ■ Only an interpretation of Sifrid's character which allows for uncourtly essentials can account for his rudeness and egoism here. (See also note 909 for a treatment of Sifrid's anger and uncooperativeness in this episode.)

It is surprising that de Boor (note to 968,1) should describe Sifrid's abuse of Hagen as "höfisch gemildert" by the use of the third person. To our knowledge, there are no general linguistic grounds for postulating such an opposition in Middle High German. In the present context, there could be few more insulting reactions than to ignore Hagen's apology (stanza 967) and to address him, the man in charge, as an impersonal and incompetent "they." It is noticeable that Hagen in his turn avoids addressing Sifrid directly in 969,1 (ir edeln ritter balt), and again when challenging him to a race (972,3–4). Compare 121,2–4, where Hagen reluctantly (119,3) addresses Sifrid with er—or perhaps avoids speaking to Sifrid, and addresses his remarks to the Burgundians.
See also note 804,2.

970,3 ▪ See note 917,3–4.

974,2–4 ▪ This scene shows to what extent it is Gunther, and not Brünnhilde, that Hagen is avenging. Gunther looks on with approval while Sifrid prostrates himself before Hagen, thus re-enacting his subservience to Gunther at Isenstein (397–8). In the next stanza (975,2–3), Sifrid offers to carry all his hunting regalia, recalling his carrying of the figure-head Gunther at Isenstein (464). Gunther's pleasure (974,4) cannot be for the practical handicap involved in all this, since it is in no one's interest that Sifrid should lose the race. Everyone knows that he will win, and be murdered. Gunther's emotion seems similar to that felt by participants in a ritual, when a significant detail is recognized as in its right place.

976,2–3 ▪ The close association in which the race to the well—which is quite unnecessary for the mechanics of the plot—involves Hagen and Sifrid is most noticeable here, where the two are paired off in a manner reminiscent of the *Gilgamesh Epic* (see note 13,2). Is perhaps the whole hunt scene a homosexual hunt, with Hagen and Sifrid the two wild boars of Kriemhilde's dream (921,2), and fatal penetration from the rear Sifrid's punishment for not caring about Worms?

976,4 ▪ See notes 909; 917,3–4.

977,4 ▪ We are reminded ominously at this moment that Sifrid is a stranger (*gast*), and yet closer in some way to the queen than anyone else (*bî dem brunnen ê; bî des brunnen vluzze*). When we add the two adjectives *küene and hêrlîch* (cf. 913,1; 917,1), we have a terrifyingly essential tableau of Sifrid's position among the Burgundians. The murder, when it comes, is almost a relief. See also note 980,1.

The Burgundians at Etzel's court are also called *geste*; see note 1999–2002.

978,3–4 ▪ See note 909.

980,1 ▪ This line possibly contains a clue to the understanding of those details of the scene which are superfluous for the actual plot. Sifrid dies, not simply because of his brashness (with the bear and over the missing wine), not simply because of his supernatural powers (he hardly seems to run in the race at all, but nevertheless appears first at the well, as if he had always been there—which of course he had, in a way, see note 977,4)—but also because of his courtesy in waiting for Gunther. One remembers that it was his courtesy in wooing Kriemhilde that helped get Sifrid into this mess, and that this courtesy involved his waiting for Gunther to marry before he himself did. It also involved offering Brünnhilde to Gunther before finally being forced to break her in himself, and this aspect is particularly close to the erotic associations of the setting here (*für die berge zuo dem brunnen* 970,3).

If the sense of *zühte* is allowed to include "restraint," (see note 496,4), then it could be his whole attempt to domesticate himself (rather than any particular act) which makes his death necessary. If the passive sense of "completed training, education" (see note 13,2) is accepted as well, then the guilt is equally with Kriemhilde, for trying to improve on nature.

981,4 ■ The ritual nature of the murder comes out in this line, as we realize the greatness of Hagen's action in offering such an unparalleled sacrifice (*grôze; helt*). His own assessment is entirely positive, as well (993). He can hardly believe that "all care and sorrow" were literally caused by Sifrid's existence, and will therefore vanish with his death. Rather, he must be rehearsing the sense of the ritual in which the Burgundians have purified themselves by sacrificing a scapegoat.

993 ■ See note 981,4.

Neither Sifrid's *hêrschaft* (line 4) nor the rosy future for the Burgundians (lines 2–3) is a political reality. It is, however, true that Hagen has set the Burgundians free to seal their own fate.

Hagen's own sense of personal liberation is also clear: the murder of Sifrid has relieved him of the burden of having to keep a close watch over his behaviour in the presence of a superman (cf. 101,1–2), and left him free to indulge himself to his heart's content in the provocation of the widow who can only fight with his own sort of means.

If one looks back from this point over Hagen's relationship to Sifrid, one notes that, although it was Hagen who was aware from the beginning of Sifrid's special powers (87–100) and Hagen who kept involving Sifrid ever deeper with the Burgundians (101, 151, 331), he nowhere shows any personal liking for Sifrid and seizes with relish on the first excuse to kill him. Even then, though, Hagen remains fascinated with what Sifrid leaves behind —Kriemhilde and the treasure—and eventually dies on their account. Could one conclude that Hagen (unwittingly) involves Sifrid with the Burgundians so as to be able to kill him off and then possess whatever it was that was so special about him?

This would help explain why, after the murder, Hagen proceeds to provoke Kriemhilde as much as he can, and why, once his cautious side has been overruled about visiting Etzel, he does everything possible to ensure total war and total destruction (cf. notes 1725,1 and 1771,3). Hagen is obsessed with the *idea* of Sifrid. The only other person so obsessed is Kriemhilde. Since they find the man himself a bit uncomfortable, all they can do is join forces to kill him, and then fight each other to the death over the (useless) remains.

See also note 1136,4.

1001,3–4 ■ By juxtaposing the two weeping women in this way, Hagen foreshadows the irony of his own death. Brünnhilde's tears (*daz Prünhilde weinen* 873,3) are strong enough to get Sifrid killed, however lightly Sifrid himself may have taken his indiscretion. Kriemhilde's tears are of no importance to Hagen, and yet they are strong enough to get him and all the Burgundians killed in the end (cf. 1100).

1010,4 ■ Kriemhilde's initial intuitive certainty as to who killed Sifrid (contrast 1012,4; 1024; 1027–29; 1033,3–4; 1044–46) is similar to that of Liudeger as to who captured his brother (cf. note 209).

See also notes 893,4; 1024.

1012,3 ■ The archaic ending of *ermorderôt* (to rhyme with *tôt*) has the slightly hollow effect of melodrama. Is there a touch of satisfaction in Kriemhilde's first reaction?
See also note 2020–23.

1024 ■ Compare 1033,4. This delaying tactic is reminiscent of *Hamlet* (e.g. "Haste me to know it, that I . . . may swoop to my revenge").
See also notes 1010,4; 1031.

1030,4 ■ Kriemhilde is not (yet) prepared to sacrifice anybody and everybody to her desire for revenge. Perhaps, also, she still has some hopes of her family, as Sifrid had when he died (996–7). Compare her pathetic reliance on her family in 1085. As yet she has no idea of the depth of her brothers' depravity, and the theft of Sifrid's treasure is still to come.
See also note 1031.

1031 ■ Kriemhilde's reasons for inaction, here and in 1024, are similar to Hamlet's. Like him, she has to wait until she loses all control of the situation before she can strike. In both cases, the inference is that "revenge" is only possible as a last resort, when all chance of a more satisfying retribution has finally disappeared. Hamlet's main worry is for his mother; Kriemhilde's only concern is for her lost husband (cf. also 1110). For both of them, revenge is a ritual duty they are loath to perform.

The extremely rational considerations put forward here by Kriemhilde are quite out of place. In fact, the Nibelungs have more chance of taking a quick revenge now, with the Burgundians guilty and divided, than ever again. By the end of the epic the original situation is forgotten, and Gunther and his men are reunited, fighting heroically for their lives against a dastardly attack. At no time during the whole tragedy are numbers decisive.
See also note 151,4.

1033,4 ■ See note 1031.

1056,2 ◼ Here, and in stanza 1068, we see the beginnings of Kriemhilde's compulsive clinging to Sifrid's remains, brought out by the use of *genieten* ("to be satiated, have one's fill") with a corpse as object, and by the emphasis on Sifrid's physical beauty (1068,2), even now that he no longer exists.

This attitude helps to explain her lack of any clear, practical motive in bringing the Burgundians to Etzel's court, and her persistent demand for restitution, however impossible. (See notes 1739,3; 1783; 2372).

1056,4 ◼ See note 343,4.

1063,4 ◼ The adverb *ringe* ("worthless," cf. 254,4) contrasts sharply with all the preceding emphasis on money. The line also reminds us of the irreplaceable loss involved in Sifrid's death, which persists in spite of all the impressive grief and mourning. By implication, the mourning is also worthless, at least as far as bringing Sifrid back to life is concerned. And then, there is something two-edged about the description of the largesse: cf. 1060,3 (*do er niht solde leben*), 1061,4 (*dem wol geliche*), 1062,4 (*nâch tôde*—i.e. not before?), 1064,4 (*die sîn ungern' enbâren*—what about the others?)

The doubts aroused by these lines are confirmed by the cynical end of the *âventiure* (1072,4). Admittedly there is no criticism implied in this line; recovering from grief is the most natural thing in the world. But funerals are designed to cover up this fact, and the whole inflated ceremony, calculated to keep Sifrid in being as long as possible, is undermined by having such a matter-of-fact observation to round it off.

The impression left of the episode is one of hollowness and insincerity. It is not so much that there was no one to mourn genuinely for Sifrid's death; the inference is rather that no one could go all the way with Kriemhilde in her effort not to accept the truth. It is doubtful whether she ever accepts it (see note 2372). Admittedly, there is a sense in which Sifrid is never finally disposed of, as Hagen bitterly complains later on (stanza 1725). But the real, positive Sifrid has gone. All that survives is Kriemhilde's perverted and obsessive sense of deprivation.

The essentially public, barbaric nature of this spectacular mourning also reflects Kriemhilde's inability to relate her loss to her own internal inconsistencies. She would like to believe that everyone mourns the departed hero (1047,1; see note 1088,3), with herself as chief mourner. Similarly, when the Burgundians arrive at Etzel's court, she wants the confrontation to be public and official, and insists on appearing in her capacity as queen (1770,4).

1078,3 ■ Although Giselher retains throughout the epic the adolescent role of younger brother, he does show some development: from taking no part in the initial encounter with Sifrid (105–127), through the making of friendly gestures on varied occasions (267, 320–22, 610, 1098), to his central function as Kriemhilde's special friend which begins here, and finally to his emergence as a fighting hero (2010–12) and his death. Giselher represents the babyish, effeminate side of the kingly figurehead (see note 126,1), not far removed from his mother's skirts (1451–53, 1491), patronized to the end by the real men (1677,4ff), protesting love for his sister even while conniving in her deception (note 1135,3—4), expressing his guilt for such weakness in fatal outbursts of spite (1213,2; 1463) directed at his father-figure Hagen, to whose strength of purpose he nevertheless rallies in the end (note 2012,1).

The history of the self-destructive inner disunity of the Burgundians which results from Hagen's high-handed murder of Sifrid and harassment of his widow can be well traced from Giselher's relations to Kriemhilde and Hagen: he leads his brothers (see note 2171) in showing (1) emotional sympathy with Kriemhilde but submission to Hagen's will so long as this is directed at turning the knife in her wounds, (2) rebellion against Hagen and active support for Kriemhilde precisely when her opportunity comes to arm herself for revenge, and (3) defense of Hagen against Kriemhilde in the final battles when such tribal solidarity is bound to lead to disaster. Is this how the death-wish operates in those who fail to grow up?

See also notes 1204,3; 1243.

1080,4 ■ See note 343,4.

1082,1 ■ Blood relationship is an important factor in the *Nibelun-genlied*, as in other mediaeval works, but it is only one loyalty among others. Hagen supports Brünnhilde against Kriemhilde, for instance, and Kriemhilde's loyalty to Sifrid is predominant in the second part of the work.

On the other hand, Kriemhilde's own personal attachment to her kinsmen is very strong—and ambivalent. She both loves and hates them. For a time she separates the two elements in her attachment and concentrates them on different people, loving Giselher (1393; see note 1397,1–2) and hating Hagen; eventually the only emotion left is a pathological hatred of them all.

Her instinctive recourse to her blood relations is clearly a nega-tive and reductive pattern. Here, it prevents her from starting a new life as widow and mother (see also note 1088,3); earlier it had brought about Sifrid's death (898). Even at the end, and after a second marriage, she is still obsessed with her family.

1085,3 ■ See note 739,2.

1088,3 ■ The purely negative nature of Kriemhilde's clinging to her family and of her mourning is underlined by her unthinking connection of the two. *mînen mâgen die mir helfen klagen* is a contradiction in terms. By mourning for Sifrid, she cuts herself off from her family; by clinging to her family, she rejects Sifrid. Complete isolation is all she gains by this action, as was fore-shadowed in 1080,4.

See also note 1082,1.

1093,3 ■ Sigemund's men are repeating Kriemhilde's excuse for delay (1024;1033). It is as if their desire for revenge is real enough, but they lack direction (1029). They also lack support, now that Kriemhilde has rejected them (and by implication Sifrid). Their frustration comes out in this rather vague threat, and in Sige-mund's uneasiness, his eagerness to leave, and finally his anger in 1092.

1097–8 ■ It is sometimes remarked that Gernot provenly knows more than he now cares to admit (cf. stanza 865). But the different attitude of the two brothers towards their innocence or guilt is a close parallel to their actual behaviour previously. Neither was in on the plot itself (926,4), but both were present when Hagen swore vengeance (stanza 865). Gernot on that occasion was silent, whereas Giselher spoke up for Sifrid (stanza 866). Now, Gernot formally (*gezogenlîchen*) claims credit for having sat on the fence, and the right (*billîche*) to be counted among Sifrid's mourners. Giselher says nothing, but is accepted without question as innocuous (*daz kint*) and as escort.

It is as if the collective responsibility of the Burgundians is confined to adult awareness. Hagen's guilt is never in doubt (993,1; 1010,4; 1131,4), and neither is Gunther's (876,1; 992,3), but Giselher is a border-line case. Hence the emphasis throughout on his *kintheit*, and his ability to make informal contact with people (Kriemhilde *passim*, and here). With Giselher's eventual death, the decision goes against him: he is classed with the rest (see notes 1078,3; 1135,3–4). Gernot's innocence is an adult affair, and only exists on paper. No one seems to pay much attention to it.

1102 ■ The isolated position within the Burgundian court which Kriemhilde now takes up is less different than one might think from that in which she first started (cf. stanzas 13–18, 138, 272–77). Her only partial assimilation represents that (feminine) aspect of the court which attracts outsiders (see notes 55,4 and 64,4). And so after a time Etzel makes an overture (in his own particular way), as Sifrid had done before.

See also note 1143,4.

1107–8 ■ There is an obvious parallel between this scene, where friendship is feigned in order to persuade Kriemhilde to send for the treasure, and the earlier one where friendship was feigned in order to persuade her to betray Sifrid (891 ff). But this time the three kings have to do some of the dirty work themselves.

1110,2 ■ See notes 1024 and 1031, and compare Claudius's advice to Hamlet ("but to persever in a course of obstinate condolement...").

1119,2–3 ■ Sifrid's personal strength which, like the possibility of its deceitful use, is associated with the *tarnkappe* (337), has died with him; what remains is the treasure—and the sword.

1120 ■ We are given a single glimpse, in this stanza, of a world in which Sifrid is seen as a rash meddler, who took away something stronger than himself (see also note 1124), which caused his death. The parallel with Gunther's fatal acquisition of Sifrid and Brünnhilde is striking, and for a moment Alberich appears as a supernatural counterpart to Dietrich.

1124 ■ This stanza states that the treasure contains great positive possibilities which neither Sifrid nor the Burgundians ever discover. Sifrid finds the magic cloak with which he deceives Brünnhilde, and is given the sword which kills so many people—from Nibelung and Schilbung to Hagen—but no one in the whole story discovers the golden wand which would have conferred mastery over the whole world.

Of course, there is no reason to suppose Sifrid would have been interested. The sword suits him better. The magic cloak he only uses to help Gunther; and Gunther is the only one who might want to sink to such an intellectualized power-symbol as a magic wand. The stanza makes it clear that Gunther is not only too weak to rival Sifrid, but also too stupid to take his one chance of being a wizard. The same thing applies to the never-ending riches of the treasure. Sifrid himself is quite unconcerned; but it is a nice hint of his great resources, which might have been used if anyone had known how to tap them.

1131,3–4 ■ Gunther and Hagen are nicely contrasted here: For Hagen's part, realistic acceptance of guilt (cf. also 873,1–2); for Gunther's, fatuous faith in convention at all costs (see also note 1204,3). Gernot and Giselher show the same attitude as Gunther (stanzas 1462–63).

1132,3 ■ *underwinden* occurs only three times in the *Nibelungenlied*, each time relating to the confiscation or taking-over of treasure. The idea (see note 531,2) of Hagen as the archetypal

treasurer, or arch-conservative, is reinforced if the three occurrences are taken together. The present one is a sort of amalgam
of the others (*slüzzel* 515,1; *alles* 1125,2; *der slüzzel aller* 1132,3).

1134,1-3 ◼ Gernot's defeatism is understandable. The Burgundians can acquire the treasure, but they cannot put it to good use:
they are indeed reduced to sinking it in the Rhine to avoid
trouble. One remembers the dilemma, and the fate, of Schilbung
and Nibelung (stanzas 89-96).

1135,3-4 ◼ Giselher's behaviour here is quite unscrupulous, for
clearly he knows what is going to happen (1140). Thus none of
the Burgundians is untainted by Hagen's *untriuwe* to Sifrid and
Kriemhilde.
    See also note 1097-8.

1136,4 ◼ This is not the only passage which makes it clear that
Hagen is not just more generally resolute than the three kings;
he specifically relishes provoking and injuring Kriemhilde. Compare his brutality towards her after Sifrid's murder (1001 and
1003-4) and his open defiance of her at Etzel's court (notes 1771,3
and 1783), as well as the fact that it is he who first arranges for
her to receive the treasure which he now takes away from her
(1107). These incidents provide the background for the personal
element in the hatred between the two which works itself out in
the last scene of the poem; for their interpretation see note 993.
    See also note 2104,1-2.

1143,4 ◼ Here begins the third disastrous "courtship from afar,"
and one wonders what it is that Sifrid, Gunther and Etzel have in
common, that they should all take the same fatal step out of their
environments. Perhaps each fancies himself in an alien context.
Sifrid at Burgundy and Gunther at Isenstein are clear enough
misfits. Etzel's delusion seems to be twofold: he sees himself as
a second Sifrid (1144,4; 1158), and also as large and extensive
enough to include and tolerate all religions (1335; 1145). In the
event, Kriemhilde turns out to be no more assimilable than Sifrid
was at Worms.

Comparison between this scene and that in which Sifrid re-
solves to woo Kriemhilde also helps explain the (exceptional) survival of the court and people of Santen. Etzel's followers see no
reason why their king should not marry Sifrid's widow, indeed
they both propose and urge this on Etzel (1143–46); and his only
consideration is whether Kriemhilde is good enough (1149). Thus
do king and people call down their fate upon themselves. By contrast Sifrid's parents fear the consequences of his wooing Kriemhilde (50–51), and Sigemund withdraws to his own kingdom without too much fuss once Sifrid is dead (1073). Apart from Sifrid,
the court and people of Santen are unambitious and self-sufficient
—and so survive.

1174,2–4. ■ Bavaria appears as a sort of no-man's-land between
the well regulated Burgundian and Hunnish kingdoms; one needs
a particular safe-guard to cross it (1429), otherwise attack is likely
(1546)—though, in fact, it only occurs under specific provocation
(1596). To some extent there is a parallel with the walt and wilde
which separate one court from another in the Arthurian epics.
They are, however, usually penetrated by an individual, whereas
Bavaria is traversed by companies.

1177–78 ■ With the Isenstein episode over and Sifrid dead, Hagen
resumes his various roles, including this one of Burgundian expert
on foreign affairs (cf. 81–82 and 1431). But whereas he only knew
Sifrid by repute (86,2), he knows both Rüdeger and Etzel's fiddlers
personally (cf. the "historical" explanation 1756).
    See also notes 55,4 and 531,2.

1195 ■ The parallel that de Boor (note to this stanza) sees between
Etzel's court and that of Arthur in the Arthurian epic may be
extended to the two kings themselves. Both are universally respected and personally ineffectual. But the parallel is highly misleading if both are not compared to Gunther and Worms. It is no
accident that both halves of the Nibelungenlied start with a long
and tedious introduction to an effete court, leading fairly quickly
to distant and disastrous courtship. Arthur, equipped with a
troublesome wife of his own, never makes this particular mistake.
    See also note 1143,4.

1199,2 ■ Whether this euphemism (*her Sîfrit sî erstorben*) is due to ignorance or delicacy, it removes the speaker so far from reality that it is difficult to take him seriously from this point on.

1200 ■ This stanza, with its tortuous correctness (underlined by the narrator: *wol gezogen was sîn muot*), and its oscillation between regal command and brotherly tentativeness, is strongly reminiscent of Gunther's discomfort when required by Brünnhilde to exert his authority over Sifrid, culminating in stanza 731. Since the discrepancy between real and pretended power is a central feature of Gunther's position, there is no need to resolve the paradox of 1200,2. Kriemhilde will do Gunther's pleasure—if she feels like it.

The last line, from which Rüdeger could reasonably infer that Gunther will refuse as soon as he can find an excuse, is inept, even in de Boor's paraphrase (see his note to this line). It will just bear the reading: "Of course, I wouldn't dream of refusing Etzel anything, unless I were really forced to," which we may assume the speaker was unsuccessfully trying to convey.

1203 ■ Compare 1205, 1210, 1212: the style is similar throughout. On the defensive here, Hagen does not wax eloquent, but repeats sullenly again and again, "I know what I know." The others, having never suffered under anything worse than their consciences, are not impressed.

1204,3 ■ Brotherly love stirs again in Gunther, as it did in stanza 1131, although the verb *sol* here, and the reference to his oath there, reflect a dutiful rather than a spontaneous attitude. It is characteristic of his insecure grasp that he should follow Hagen and betray Kriemhilde's sisterly trust on the earlier occasion, when she was still open to reconciliation, only to uphold her claims against Hagen now it is too late. His persistent belief in the force of natural ties, which he has himself casually broken, shows a quite exceptional inability to differentiate, and goes some way to account for his blandness in the making of tragic blunders.

The same applies to his brothers Gernot and Giselher, whose

righteous denunciations of Hagen (1208–1213) are an unpleasant
contrast to their earlier silence and inaction (1134; 1135).
  See also note 1078,3.

1206,1–3 ▪ Compare 1211. In the event, the rashness of the three
kings and their anxiety to believe in the reconcilation with their
sister prevents their exercizing such caution (1460–70). They
show absolutely no sense of responsibility on either occasion; all
they want is to ease their consciences, to "feel good" once again

1220,2 ▪ This absolute formulation of Kriemhilde's resolve to
love no one, with the particular cause momentarily suppressed,
recalls her attitude before she ever met Sifrid (15–18). The parallelism and the differences between her two marriages are thus
formally underlined, but at the same time a permanent characteristic of Kriemhilde is brought out which connects her with
Brünnhilde. Her reluctance to be plucked is a paler and more
socially conditioned reflection of Brünnhilde's superhuman virginity. There is a similar relation between Gunther's and Sifrid's
masculinity, in love and in war; so that from this point of view,
Sifrid and Brünnhilde appear as embodiments of the absolutes
which Gunther and Kriemhilde foolishly try to import into their
compromise-ridden society. The actual physical importations
Hagen manages to deal with in Part I, but the things in Gunther
and Kriemhilde which called them up are still there, and are
finally too much for him.
For the force of *minnen*, see notes 3,1; 1250,3.

1243 ▪ Here, as always, Giselher's special relationship with
Kriemhilde is more a pious hope than a reality. In spite of the
insistently individual formulation (*mir ist geseit; und wilz gelou-
ben; so dunket mich; swaz ander iemen râte*), he is merely repeating what the entire Burgundian court (except Hagen) un-
thinkingly accepts.
  See also note 1078,3.

1250,3 ▪ The impossibility of these Burgundian hopes is brought
out if *minnen* is given its full force of "love," here and 1254,1.

(For another fond hope, see note 1255,3, on *ergetzen*). The Burgundians perform a typically political *non sequitur*: "it would
be a good thing if Kriemhilde loved Etzel; therefore it must be
possible for Kriemhilde to love Etzel," and they advise her
accordingly. By this stanza, they are already beginning to prevail
on Kriemhilde, but it is revealing that her first motive for considering the proposal is the acquisition of power (stanza 1247).
Hagen was right, and the emptiness of all their talk of *minnen*
must be apparent. But if they admitted to themselves that her
only motive for marrying would have to be political and economic, and that "love" was out of the question, they would no
longer be able to persuade her so earnestly to encompass their
own destruction.

On the meaning of MHG *minnen*, see note 3,1. The word may
occasionally approach NHG "heiraten" (see de Boor, note to this
line), but its centre is personal and emotional (with 1205,3 and
1207,3 compare 1220,2). That Rüdeger should use *minnen* when
trying to win Kriemhilde round (1235,1, cf. 1232,1) supports this
view; and when the poet wants to be unambiguous, he has *nemen*
for the bare fact of marriage (1202,4; 1219,4).

1255,3 ■ Rüdeger's offer of compensation (*ergetzen*) is apparently
decisive for Kriemhilde. She accepts immediately, first taking the
precaution of making Rüdeger commit himself specifically to her
cause. The process of *ergetzen* may come close to "revenge" in
some contexts (like NE "to get one's own back"), but it remains
essentially a wider, more comprehensive and impossible demand.
It is used repeatedly in the *Nibelungenlied* to refer to compensation for Kriemhilde's loss of Sifrid. Compensation is promised her
by Giselher (1049,3; 1080,3; 1208,3; 1244,1), Gernot (1049,3),
Gere (1215,4) and Rüdeger (1234,1 and here), the last promise tip-
ping the scales in favour of remarriage. The promises are empty,
just as the political attitude to *minnen* (note 1250,3) was empty.
Kriemhilde's marriage to Etzel is no compensation; all it does is
give her the power to make her demands more destructive. When
Hagen confronts her on arrival at Etzelnburg, she is still demanding restitution (1739), and when she finally receives him as
prisoner from Dietrich, she can still hope for *ergetzen* (2354,3;

2355,3). After one last demand (*gelt* 2372,1), she gives up and takes revenge instead.

The only other character in the book who shows a comparable concern with loss and repayment is Dietrich. He seems to want compensation from the Burgundians (2336,3; 2339,4), and shows understanding of Kriemhilde's demands on Hagen (2355,3). This rather surprising alignment raises the question of what Dietrich and Kriemhilde might have in common. Their behaviour is dissimilar, with Dietrich exemplifying restraint, and Kriemhilde extremity. They are, it is true, both forced into similar positions; both must survive (for a while at least) the loss of everything they value, and everything that gives them any power to influence others (see Dietrich's lament, stanzas 2319–20). Both rebel against survival and wish they could die (Kriemhilde 1056,3–4; Dietrich 2323,4).

There seems to be nothing in their actions which makes a common fate necessary. Dietrich does nothing analogous to Kriemhilde's marriage of Etzel. And yet the bracketing is not fortuitous. If we go one stage further back, a basic similarity underlying their greatly divergent careers becomes apparent. Both are initially determined to remain detached (Kriemhilde stanza 17; Dietrich, stanzas 1901 and 1992). Neither succeeds. Continuity is provided in that we leave Dietrich in much the same situation as Kriemhilde had been left in just after Sifrid's death. Whatever his solution (and it will hardly be the same as Kriemhilde's), his problem, like hers, is connected with the impossibility of non-involvement and the irrevocability of his loss.

1256,4 ▪ This undertaking is the basis of Rüdeger's later dilemma. He never does anything wrong, and no doubt he deserves our sympathy; but there is something irritating about his inability to see anything dangerous in any situation. He seems to take conventional values at their face value. Add together obligingness (here), hospitality (âventiure 27) and then loyalty, and his fate is assured.

The much debated problem whether Rüdeger is aware of exactly what his promise means to Kriemhilde is irrelevant. It is precisely his eagerness to engage himself on all sides without being aware of what is involved that proves his undoing. And not his alone—though if Etzel had wanted to be cautious, he should have chosen a different ambassador.

See also notes 2142; 2166,3–4; 2196–97.

1259–60 ▪ Thoughts of revenge occur to Kriemhilde here, but tentatively, in the form of a question, and more as a possible argument in favour of marrying Etzel than as a clear-cut need. They are immediately followed by other more positively formulated advantages: power (1260,2) and wealth, with its opportunities for generosity (1260,3). The self-persuasive monologue is rounded off with a repetition of her "loss and restitution" obsession, first stated immediately after Sifrid's death, and taken up again when she confronts Hagen at Etzel's court (stanza 1739).

See also note 1255,3.

1276,2–3 ▪ It is in keeping with the ominously ironic style of the *Nibelungenlied* (see Burghart Wachinger, *Studien zum Nibelungenlied: Vorausdeutungen, Aufbau, Motivierung* [Tübingen, 1960], especially pp. 24–27) that statements such as this one of Kriemhilde's should reverberate on other levels. Kriemhilde's "loss" is a complex thing, and she is conscious of now one aspect, now another. The absolute, irreplaceable quality of what she once had can be heard in this speech, and is taken up in the final scene of the epic. After a cry such as this, all talk of regaining the treasure, or Sifrid, is merely a rhetorical reference to the enormity of her loss, and Hagen's guilt (2372). The Burgundian talk of *ergetzen* sounds hollow in this context.

See also note 1255,3.

1277,4 ▪ As usual, Gunther is not very much in evidence when something unpleasant has to be done. The narrator here reminds us of his existence, and at the same time emphasizes his characteristically passive part in the proceedings. Compare 667 and 674, when Sifrid subdues his wife for him. Compare also 974,4, where the formulation is almost exactly the same, and the reminder of Gunther just as unexpected and revealing.

1312,4 ◼ *ellende* sounds ominous this early, emphasizing the forced, second-best nature of Kriemhilde's second marriage. From now on, the word is applied to all the strangers at Etzel's court: Burgundians, Rüdeger and Dietrich, none of whom has a future among the Huns.

See also notes 1526,2, 1572,3–4, and 1999–2002.

1320,3 ◼ The journey from Worms to Etzel's court is contrasted sharply with that to Isenstein: the one familiar, even intimate, the other vague and mysterious. If the poet's presumed Austrian homeland suggests a genetical explanation of this contrast, its significance for the finished work—the distinction between the two directions in which the Burgundians move—is also worthy of attention. The overall effect here is one of cosiness and suffocation, relieved by rare ominous flashes, as 1328,1; 1330,4. Concentration, reduction, regression even; in contrast to their earlier distension.

On the precise routes taken by the various travellers between Worms and Etzel's court, see further A. T. Hatto's translation (1965), pp. 396 ff. Interestingly enough, it appears that even in the presumed poet's home country these routes are not entirely contemporary or realistic: here as elsewhere rationality was not all-important.

1335 ◼ See note 1368.

1358,3–4 ◼ This picture of Etzel with his mouth watering is strongly reminiscent of Gunther at a similar stage in his career (cf. 528,1; 624,4ff.; and note 296). This feature, which is absent from Sifrid's courtship, is perhaps a symptom of political marriages. It certainly makes one wonder whether Etzel's unsubtle reduction of Kriemhilde to an object of his lust is as inappropriate to her real function in his life as Gunther's treatment of Brünnhilde was. They both, in their animal appetite, bite off more than they can chew. Even though Kriemhilde causes no trouble to Etzel in bed, she is finally disastrous to his pretensions, and he might well have echoed Gunther's heartfelt: *want ich hân den übeln tiuvel heim ze hûse geladen* (649,2). There are other parallels between Kriemhilde and Brünnhilde (see note 1220,2).

1368 ■ Several times the narrator invites us to contrast Kriemhilde's first husband with her second; as if personal strength were symbolized by the treasure Sifrid wins single-handed, and public position by the vast hordes, Christian and heathen, who owe allegiance to, but are hardly dominated by, Etzel. Compare the revealing account of the power structure of Etzel's dominions in stanza 1335, the overt reference to Etzel's superiority over Sifrid in numbers (1365,3–4), and Hagen's sneer at Etzel's real inferiority (note 2020–23).

For a fuller treatment of Etzel's inadequacies, see Gottfried Weber, *Das Nibelungenlied: Problem und Idee* (Stuttgart, 1963), pp. 75–83.

1370,4 ■ The conventional exaggeration here is treated with some irony and detachment. Compare 1573,4, where a gross understatement has a similar undermining effect.

1394,1 ■ The narrator designates the victory of Kriemhilde's hatred over her love for her brothers as devilish; Dietrich calls her a devil when she reveals her intentions (1748,4); and so does Hagen at the end (2371,4). The dramatic effect of Hagen's last defiant insult is perhaps reduced by the two preceding passages, but the stages in Kriemhilde's degeneration are indicated more clearly than would otherwise be the case. The word used each time is *vâlant, vâlandinne*.[10]

Hagen and Gunther have a similar reaction to Brünnhilde's un-Burgundian activities at Isenstein, but for her they use the word *tiuvel* (438,4; 442,2; 450,4; 649,2). For them, apparently, hell is

[10] H. Linke, "Uber den Erzähler im Nibelungenlied und seine künstlerische Funktion," *Germanisch-Romanische Monatsschrift*, Vol. XLI, Neue Folge Vol. X (1960), p. 379, takes the narrator's remark here as evidence of his "courtly" incomprehension of the "heroic" characters in his story. He puts particular emphasis on the phrase *ich waene*, as showing real doubt and uncertainty. For a more sophisticated treatment of such formulae, see A. T. Hatto, " 'Ine Weiz' . . . Diplomatic Ignorance on the Part of Mediaeval German Poets," *German Studies presented to L. A. Willoughby*, Oxford (1952), pp. 98–107.

peopled with women they do not understand, or cannot manage.
See also note 438,4.

1395,3 ▪ Kriemhilde hardly tries to make the best of things. Admittedly she did object to marrying a heathen (1248), but it was for political rather than religious reasons. Heathens are obviously second-rate citizens in the *Nibelungenlied*, as the final battle shows. Etzel himself is a poor substitute for Sifrid, and it is true that Kriemhilde was forced into taking him after having Sifrid stolen from her. This marriage is a relegation, and she feels it as such.
See also note 1312,4, on *ellende*.

1397,1–2 ▪ Possibly one should print a comma instead of a full stop after *mîn*, giving a construction similar to that in stanza 1; then Kriemhilde would obviously be confusing her attempted distinction between the relatives she loves and those she hates. The use of punctuation regrettably forces editors to resolve such points for their readers rather than leave them open (cf. notes to 152 and 385–6).

Even with the inserted full stop, the pressure of the verse form is still towards reading the two lines as a simple parallel, without any "but" or "whereas" understood. Such a reading would pair *den getriuwen* with *die mir dâ leide tâten*, adding the bitterness of line 2 to the conventional formulation of line 1. Some degree of pairing is also implied between *den getriuwen* and the plural *mînen vîenden* (1396,3); indeed the whole passage (from 1391,4) reveals that when Kriemhilde remembers her kinsmen, she experiences ambivalent emotions which she tries to straighten out, but with only partial success.
See also notes 1082,1 and 1716,2.

1398,4 ▪ Kriemhilde's queenly activities and personal success at Etzel's court do not indicate an expansion but a contraction of her personality; she achieves more now that she is concentrating on a single goal.

1407,3 ■ The social standing of minstrels in the *Nibelungenlied* is not simple. Werbel and Swemmelin are eminent enough to convey an invitation to a feast—a different matter from an offer of marriage—and to have a retinue of twenty-four distinguished warriors (*recken* 1409,1); but they are described only as squires (*knappen* 1436,4) and do not actually eat with Gunther on arrival in Worms (1450). One may well wonder why their minstrelsy is so emphasized (cf. 1433,2).

Volker's position is different, in that he is described as a warrior who just happens to be able to play the fiddle (but see also 1477, note). His dual nature provides an opportunity for the overworked "fiddling=killing" metaphor (1966; 1976,2; 2001–7), and forms a contrast (cf. 2001) to the strictly non-combatant, harmless Werbel (1963 ff.). On the other hand, the mere fact of common minstrelsy makes Werbel and Swemmelin to some extent anticipate Volker's more important role (see note 1673,3).

1409,4–1413,3 ■ In spite of line 1409,4, Kriemhilde does not actually speak privately to the messengers until after Etzel has finished (1413,2–3). Nevertheless, the occurrence of this line before Etzel starts makes it impossible to hear his confident invitation and bland assertion of happiness (e.g. 1411,4), without being conscious of Kriemhilde's darker motives. When she eventually speaks, she takes up the theme of marital bliss, but negatively, and with a clear intention to deceive (1415,2–3: "don't tell them you ever saw me miserable").

1419–20 ■ This reminder that, if Hagen stays behind, Kriemhilde's whole plan for revenge will fail, gives special point to the argument that ensues between Hagen and the three kings when the messengers arrive at Worms. *Could* Hagen have stayed behind?

1459,1 ■ Hagen can still use the *wir* form here, associating the three kings in his deed; but during the scene they reject the association, all three using the *wir* form to exclude Hagen (1460–70). Hagen reacts with *ir* (1471 ff.).

1461,3 ■ cf. 425,3. The repetition of phrase, coinciding as so often in oral-formulaic style with a repetition of situation, draws attention to the fact that Gunther is threatened a second time by a woman, but on this occasion cannot look to Sifrid to save him.

1463,3 ■ cf. 174,3 and note 886,1. But of course there is a difference between a figure-head staying behind, and his leading warrior doing so.

1465 ff. ■ Rumold is something of a caricature. He puts himself on a level with Hagen (1466; see also note 343,4), then goes on to give a parodistically down-to-earth version of Hagen's cautious advice (cf. especially 1467–68). This aspect of Rumold was foreshadowed by the narrator in stanza 777.

1468,4 ■ Rumold can dismiss heroism (*wâgen den lîp*) as childish, just as Dietrich dismisses the heroic "Trutzrede" as old-womanish (see note 2345,2). Both evidently stand outside the arena in which the inevitable tragedy is played out.

1476,1 ■ Once the close, ruling alliance between Hagen and the three kings has been disrupted, lesser figures have a part to play. The first such is Rumold, representing the cautious side of Hagen. The second, more important, is Volker, representing Hagen's recklessness, his conviction that the reputation of the Burgundian court stands and falls with its hostility to Kriemhilde. Rumold's support fails to win the three kings over to Hagen's caution; without Volker's support Hagen would have found it more difficult, if not impossible, to involve them in his bitter feud, to make them accept his glorious, but fatal solution (cf. also 1584,4).

In a sense, both are caricatures of what Hagen stands for. The cook-figure is an expressive image for the intensely practical mind of Hagen. The bloody fiddler has something of the wild élan that Hagen shows once the fight is inevitable.

See also notes 1465 ff.; 1477; 1673,3.

1477 ■ There is a hint of embarrassment about this stanza, in which the narrator tries to explain away a (presumably traditional) feature which raises no problems within the epic but which might presumably have disturbed his contemporary audience: that a fiddler can be a noble lord. After the Danube crossing, at the point where Volker's role really gets under way, he is introduced a second time (1584). No embarrassment is visible there, but three relevant facts about his role are listed in as many lines: (1) that he is a great fighter, (2) that he has a pretty wit and always speaks his mind, and (3) that whatever Hagen does seems good to him.

See also notes 1407,3; 1928,3–4.

1485 ■ Gunther's permission (*erloubte*, line 1) seems to count for very little in this matter, and one wonders what can have gone wrong with Brünnhilde that he should be so conspicuously excluded from all arrangements concerning her. If she were really likely to suffer from seeing the messengers, her husband might be expected to be the first to know about this. On the other hand, if the phrase *daz was ir liebe getân* (line 4) is a euphemism designed to conceal the embarrassment of the Burgundians at the thought of letting her see the messengers, then the suspicion is aroused that she and Gunther do not always agree.

Looked at either way, she is no longer at the centre of the court. Her position as queen of Burgundy seems even less influential than that of Rüdeger's wife, for instance, and her untouchability is reminiscent of Kriemhilde before her marriage. The queen mother Uote is allowed to see the messengers, but Gernot emphasizes that this is because of her personal tie with Kriemhilde (1452,3–4).

See also note 1492,4.

1492,4 ■ The narrator's explanation draws attention to an apparent inconsistency in the messengers' behaviour, and suggests a difference between Gunther's largesse and Uote's presents. That difference is expressed by *mit triuwen*, which Bartsch translates as "aus aufrichtiger Gesinnung," and which de Boor paraphrases more specifically as: "aus Dankbarkeit für gute Nachricht." But the goodness of the news is not the point. The true contrast is between Gunther's perfunctory pretentiousness, and Uote's genuine feeling for Kriemhilde her daughter. This allows *mit triuwen* to be given its usual meaning. Uote is not a political figure. Gunther is very little else.

The two situations are nicely characterized by their respective effect on the messengers. In one case, embarrassment, fear of offending Etzel, and the bother of carrying the stuff (1490,4). In the other, the traditional pleasure of messengers when rewarded (1492,4).

1503,2–4 ◼ The irony inherent in any exemplary, static, complacently self-regarding set of values is now beginning to show more openly. Once we know that Kriemhilde intends to use one of the most exemplary of all Burgundian conventions as an instrument to break the society, the narrator can rely on our catching the ominous undertones in lines such as the last in this stanza. The effect works back on *wie rehte minneclîche*, referring to a typical facet of Kriemhilde's public persona, which by now only Etzel could possibly take at its face value. The effect was also led up to by the blatant irony of *Hagenen bin ich waege* (1502,3), and by Kriemhilde's reference to her *hôhe muot* (1502,4), which is a clear echo of Sifrid's eagerness for battle with the Saxons (181,4).

The suggestion that Etzel might also be unconvincing under strain is developed later (1982,4; 2021–2).

See also 1716,2 and 2122,4, where the ideas of "Kriemhilde's welcome" and "Kriemhilde's hospitality" are played with.

1523,1–2 ◼ This mention of "Nibelungs" is an obscure anticipation of stanza 1526. The phrase *mit in*, which presumably goes back to *die snellen Burgorden* (stanza 1522), suggests that a separate detachment is meant. The reference to "1,000 coats of mail" (1523,2) points the other way. It is apparently a reference to stanza 1478, and suggests that these are the thousand Burgundian warriors that Hagen collected. On the other hand, the phrase clearly evokes the thousand Nibelungs that Sifrid brought back from Isenstein (597,4). At a later stage the narrator makes it clear that only 1,000 knights take part in this expedition all told (apart from Hagen's own group of sixty, cf. stanzas 1573 and 1647); by then, apparently, the identification of Gunther's and Sifrid's men, first adumbrated in the present stanza (1523), can be taken for granted.

See note 1526,2.

1526,2 ■ This is the first unambiguous(but see also note 1523,1–2) occurrence of *Nibelunge* applied as a name to the Burgundians. In documenting this and the later occurrences, Bartsch (*Nibelungenlied Wörterbuch*) remarks that they become Nibelungs after they have taken possession of the Nibelung treasure. This is true, but leaves a considerable time-lag to be explained. The thing that happens *immediately* before the name-change is their departure from Burgundy (1522).

In the first half of the epic, the name is applied to the two princes, Schilbung and Nibelung, whom Sifrid kills, and to their followers (inherited with other possessions from the founder of the dynasty, also called Nibelung?), whom Sifrid acquires (87–99). Sifrid later chooses a thousand of these to take to Isenstein, and they are still called *Nibelunge*, naturally enough, since they come from *Nibelunge*, a distant and enigmatic place (501,3; 502,3; 597,4; 617,4; cf. 484,4). It is a reasonable assumption that Sifrid keeps them in his retinue after this, bringing them back to Burgundy, and finally back to his own country. This could account for the fact that Sifrid's men are always liable to be called Nibelungs in Burgundy (e.g. 1015,2; 1030,2; 1058,4; 1095,4), although in each case they have been brought straight from his own country, and contain at least 100 Netherlanders (761). It is as if Sifrid's men are Nibelungs by definition. This would mean that to be a Nibelung is to be mysterious, magical, mythological. Perhaps this is why Sifrid, at his least mythological (i.e. just after marrying Kriemhilde), returns to Santen in the Netherlands (708,4), only to re-emerge, when needed for ritual sacrifice, at Nibelunge (739,2–3). Even Sigemunde is attracted there for a moment (754,3), although he goes home quietly after Sifrid's death. (See also note 739,2.)

Hagen's Nibelungs have a strikingly similar origin and career. They too are chosen, a thousand in number (1472,3; 1478), to be taken on a journey. Like Sifrid's men, they become a close-knit and threatened group at a foreign court. Once Sifrid is dead,

Kriemhilde sends his men back home. When Hagen's men arrive at Etzel's court, she tries to produce a parallel outcome. If they give up Hagen, she will let them go home (2104); but, in the event, they stick together and suffer the fate that Sifrid's Nibelungs escaped.

Kriemhilde's rather puzzling refusal to let the earlier band take revenge, and no doubt get themselves killed in the process (see note 1031), makes more sense if her (unconscious) resolve was to get the Burgundians in the same exposed, friendless condition, and let them feel what it was like. At all events, that is just what she does. She is unfortunate by then in being tied to both camps. Earlier, family loyalty had destroyed her marriage; now she uses marital loyalty to destroy her family. As it happens, the two are equally matched; Hunnish solidarity against the intrusive group is answered so well by Burgundian solidarity that it is the Nibelungs who occupy the hall, and the Huns who are excluded.

Nibelung, then, means something like: "mythological, unreal, not of this society." As applied to the Burgundians, it also means "as good as dead" (compare the ferrying across the Danube, and Hagen's certainty of death afterwards). This cannot hold for Sifrid's men, but it is striking that on two occasions they are put through an "awakening scene" (when Sifrid calls for them, 502–3, and when he is murdered, 1015–18), reminiscent of the slumbering armies of the dead (e.g. Charlemagne's), found in folklore.

1541 ▪ This question of Hagen's shows that up to now he has only been certain of the danger represented by Kriemhilde's enmity. Certainty of destruction comes with crossing the Danube.

1551,1 ▪ Compare 259,1 and note.
   See also note 1572,3–4.

1572,3–4 ▪ There are many strange and apparently unnecessary details in this scene, some of them (like this) reminiscent of Sifrid, Sifrid also is a sort of ferryman on the way to Isenstein, is too rich to render service or accept gifts (259,1; 556,4), yet does both for the sake of marriage (cf. 1554,1), and is killed by Hagen, somewhat to the discomfiture of the three kings (1567–9). Is the point of the scene to show Hagen still behaving (on a small scale) in a manner parallel to and reminiscent of his earlier crucial acts? Certainly, after the ferryman's death, as after that of Sifrid, Hagen openly controls the destiny of the Burgundians.

He also becomes the ferryman, and in a sense supersedes Sifrid. His formulation (1570,2–3) *ich gedenke daz ich was der aller beste verge, den man bî dem Rîne vant* is a new and disturbing thought. Why did he say nothing about this when Sifrid offered to ferry them to Isenstein? Are we to understand that he resented being usurped so early, or does he perhaps mean that he *had been* the best, till Sifrid arrived to outclass him?

In any case, murdering the ferryman a second time lifts a load from his mind, and he can now use Sifrid's favourite phrase: *ja trûwe ich* (1570,4; see note 55,4).

The twin facts, that the Burgundians become Nibelungs (cf. note 1526,2) and that Hagen takes over certain characteristics of Sifrid, also for instance wielding his sword (cf. notes 1783 and 1657,3), throw looming shadows over any attempt to interpret the poem. They can be related to Hagen's need to persecute Kriemhilde after Sifrid's death (cf. note 993) and to Kriemhilde's parallel concentration upon Hagen (as a substitute for Sifrid). Obviously Sifrid and his Nibelungs form to some extent a single composite symbol ("the Sifrid myth"), which is both attractive and inimical to the Burgundians. And whereas Kriemhilde initially wants Sifrid but gets Sifrid and his Nibelungs, so later she wants Hagen but gets Hagen and *his* Nibelungs.

Perhaps Hagen and the Burgundians get irrevocably infected by contact with Sifrid, so that the Sifrid myth can only be expunged by destroying the whole society? This would explain why all Burgundians, and all who come into contact with them, become *ellende* (cf. note 1312,4), like the Nibelungs, supernatural, out of place, not tolerable to any society, doomed.

1583,4 ▪ The flooded Danube is the chief obstacle on the Burgundians' journey from Worms to Etzel's court—and the smashing of the boat reveals the crossing of it as a symbolic act. It is the point of no return: previously all had expected to survive, gradually all accept their own destruction. Previously also, all had wanted to survive, and had appeared on occasion as cautious, treacherous and cowardly; henceforth they further their own doom, and appear rash, noble, heroic. That it is Hagen alone who ferries them across is revealing for his role.

1584 ◼ See notes 1476,1 and 1477.

1613 ◼ Hagen's heroism is based on solidarity and the possibility of help from his friends and relations. Compare Dankwart's appeal (1952,1–2). This is, of course, the strength of the Burgundians, and at the same time the cause of their annihilation. Contrast Sifrid's essentially single-handed valour in the Saxon war, and Kriemhilde's very Burgundian mistake in asking Hagen to protect him (see note 898,1–2).

Although Hagen eventually emerges as the toughest of the Burgundians, he is individually weaker than Volker (1768,2). Indeed, his most effective actions arise from his close partnership with the fiddler, where Volker supplies the wild exuberance, and Hagen the caution and endurance (see note 1476,1).

1631,3–4 ◼ Much has been written about the literary source of this episode[11]; very little about its function in the work. Ekkewart is a Burgundian margrave who has, ever since Kriemhilde's first marriage, been particularly attached to her, whom he accompanied both to Santen and to Etzel's court (700,4; 1283–84). His intimacy with Kriemhilde and his allegiance to her brothers may explain his knowledge of her plans and his desire to warn the Burgundians (1635,3). And he could not have foreseen that Hagen would have anticipated danger and so would brush aside his warning (stanza 1636). But what of his curious relationship with Rüdeger? As Kriemhilde's follower, Sifrid's dependent (1633,3),

---

[11] Friedrich Panzer, *Das Nibelungenlied: Entstehung und Gestalt* (Stuttgart, 1955), pp. 391 ff., sees Ekkewart as an amalgam of the loyal Eckart who sits before the Venusberg and warns against entry, the Eckehart of the Dietrich-cycle, who watches over and avenges the Harlungs, and the historical Margrave Eckehart II of Meissen whose statue can still be seen in Naumburg cathedral. He then concludes a purely genetical study with the comment: "Ich nehme an, dass mit diesen Darlegungen eine befriedigende Erklärung unseres Auftrittes gegeben ist" (p. 395).

Rüdeger's sentry, and warner of the Burgundians, he seems to symbolize the confused loyalties of the final scenes, and especially of Rüdeger himself. Rüdeger's vulnerability to Hagen is particularly stressed here (1631,4; 1632,4; 1633,4), and foreshadows the surrender of his shield, again to Hagen, once the fight is on.

The fact that Ekkewart has erred by falling asleep seems to imply more than can easily be explained. Parallels could be sought in other works. An obvious one is the way in which Gilgamesh loses immortality by falling asleep—and note that he too, like Ekkewart, is given a second chance by his awakener.

1634 ▣ Hagen's generous treatment of Ekkewart foreshadows Rüdeger's later generosity to Hagen (2196). The later episode is pure magnanimity to a respected foe, caught at a momentary disadvantage. Such a description would not exhaust the present encounter. Ekkewart is a rather ridiculous figure, and there is no indication that he has earned Hagen's respect. The tone of 1634,4 is patronizing, while stanza 1636 is, at the least, impolite. In these surroundings, the magnanimous gesture, followed immediately by a gratuitous gift of rings, becomes a display of confidence so unshakable as to be near to contempt. Hagen never for a moment risks his own safety by his action. Rüdeger actually gets himself killed by his indiscriminate generosity (2220,1).

See also note 2196–97.

1647,3–4 ▪ The contrast between *ritter* and *knehte* is that between fully qualified fighting-men ("knights") and those not so qualified (the young squires and servants who wait on the knights, 1897,3–4). But the phrasing is misleading in implying a similar hierarchic contrast between *ritter* and *recken*: they are just two of five barely distinguishable words for fighting-men in the poem (cf. *helt*, *degen*, *man*). All the same, the choice of *recken* here is not quite arbitrary: in other places, too, *recke* is used to describe a small band of warriors distinct from the general crowd (161,3; 171,3; 542,1; 1409,1; cf. 341,1).

Also, *ritter* is not used in statements of allegiance, and these sixty *recken* are specifically Hagen's men (cf. the parallel stanza 1573). All the other four words for fighting-men are found in this sort of statement (*die Dietrîches man* 1354,1; *ir Etzelen helde* 2092,2; *die Sîfrides degene* 1046,4), though of course *man* more commonly than the others, since it pairs in this sense with *hêrre* (386,3). But one of the four, *helt*, refers more typically to a single individual and his provenance (*der helt von Burgonden* 1736,4); compare the fact, noted by Bartsch, that Sifrid is commonly described as *der helt* without further qualification (88,1), almost anticipating "the hero" of modern fiction.

The adjectives associated with the remaining three words (excluding *ritter* and *helt*) suggest that (1) *man* is in itself fairly colourless, allowing a wide variety of adjectives (though especially *küene* and *waetlich*), (2) *degen*, while normally occurring with much the same adjectives as the others, shows a slight tendency to frivolity, being for instance the only one found with *zierlîch*, and (3) *recke* alone occurs quite frequently with adjectives expressing isolation, such as *ellende, unkunt* and *vremde.*

Since *recke* thus retains in the *Nibelungenlied* some traces of its earlier meaning of "lone hero" or "exile," but can nevertheless indicate allegiance, it is perhaps well-suited for small bands of fighting-men attached to such a leader as Hagen. Gottfried Weber's attempts to lend it metaphysical significance ("cut off from the grace of Christ") seem to us misguided, and his statistical tables on *ritter, helt* and *recke* too elementary to be much help (*Das Nibelungenlied: Problem und Idee* [Stuttgart, 1963], pp. 151 ff. and 212 ff.).

1656 ff. ■ The relaxed, idyllic atmosphere of the interlude in Bechelaren has frequently been noted as a last picture of pleasantly harmonious courtly society before everything breaks down.

The same atmosphere can also be related to Rüdeger's peculiar position. He has no lands, and no political function. For him, hospitality (stanza 1648), generosity (stanza 1704), greeting kiss (stanza 1665–6) and marriage of his daughter (stanza 1685) are, if not ends in themselves, at most a means of buttressing his own personal security (cf. the narrator's comment in stanza 1704 and notes 1256,4; 2150,3).

1657,3 ■ The reason for this special greeting is less interesting than its effect of isolating Hagen among the Burgundians. This isolation by greeting becomes more obtrusive in 1738,3, and it pushes Hagen more quickly into the provocative posture he assumes before Kriemhilde (1781 ff.). The whole pattern is parallel to Sifrid's isolation from among the Burgundians by Brünnhilde's special greeting (419–20; cf. also note 511,4), and reinforces the impression that Hagen has in some way taken over Sifrid's function.

See also note 1572,4.

1673,3 ■ Volker's light-heartedness in killing accords with his role of a fighting hero who has had no previous relationships with anybody, who is unencumbered by history, who has taken no part in the deep and devious jostling for position that characterizes peace-time. Only coming to the fore as the final battles approach, he is reminiscent of such allegorical figures as the fiddler in Keller's *Romeo und Julia auf dem Dorfe* or Death in Cocteau's *Black Orpheus*. (From this point of view the repetitious killing-playing metaphor is perhaps after all just bearable: see note 1407,3).

See also notes 1476,1 and 1613.

1686,3 ■ See note 2196–97.

1694–96 ■ There is a splendid blandness about the narrator's style in reporting Rüdeger's bounty (cf. especially 1694,4 in its context).

See also note 2196–97.

1701 ■ See note 2196–97.

1716,2 ■ A pretty picture, and in the best tradition, as the narrator points out. But the choice of this particular formula (*so friunt nâch friunden tuont*), with its reminiscence of Sifrid's naïve remark (*alsô man vriunden sol* 748,2), and with its internal repetition, concentrates attention on the highly ambiguous nature of Kriemhilde's feelings and expectations at this moment. It is not that *vriunt* is in itself ambiguous, although it refers to a

category of intimate associates which does not coincide completely with either "blood-relations" or "friends"; the ambiguity is really in the phrase structure *alsô* . . . *man tuot*. Is this a convention that is never broken, or one which only a Kriemhilde could break?
See also notes 1397,1–2 and 1717.

1717 ■ The powerfully ironic effect of line 1 is reinforced, first by Etzel's emphasis on *liebe* and *lachen* immediately before, against a brooding background of impending doom; secondly by the contrast with *mîner leide* (line 4); and thirdly by the conscious ambiguity in Kriemhilde's use of *vreuden*. Perhaps Kriemhilde is herself misled at this moment, in that she is so taken up with the success of the vengeful scheme that she cannot foresee her own grisly conclusion. But, if so, then Etzel is twice fooled, in that he takes these references to happiness in their most conventional sense. He does not realize that Kriemhilde's joy at the approach of her family is akin to Sifrid's exultation when he surveyed the enemy in front of him (cf. note 194).[12]
After the first line of this stanza, we are ready for ambiguities. In line 1, the stress may be put on *mîner*, so that Kriemhilde's remark looks backward rather than forward, contrasting her joy with Etzel's. Or, if a forward connection is insisted on, one may wonder if Kriemhilde's pathological state does not rejoice in the prospect of a bigger blood-bath than she had expected (2086,1). Or does she even half wish the Burgundians to triumph—and save her from herself?
A third possibility also cannot be ruled out; that she is saying (or thinking) this as an encouragement to the Huns. The new shields and armour are prospective booty, and constitute a reward for loyalty additional to the money she promises in line 3.

1725,1 ■ This defiant refusal to pay attention to Dietrich's warning sets the tone for Hagen's later provocation of Kriemhilde

---

[12] Burghart Wachinger, *Studien zum Nibelungenlied: Vorausdeutungen, Aufbau, Motivierung* (Tubingen, 1960), p. 64n, notes this parallel, and relates the situation to a motif (joy at the approach of battle) found elsewhere, including the *Song of Roland*.

(1738 ff.; 1781 ff.) and Etzel (1918; 1960 ff.). Compare also his rejection of the one opportunity to sort things out in time (1861–65).

1726,1. ■ Dietrich's magnificent unconcern for Hagen's great crime (see note 981,4) is part of his essential detachment.
See also notes 1733; 2345,2; 2312,4.

1733 ■ Hagen's murder of Sifrid has now become a legendary act adding to his stature, much as Sifrid's past deeds impressed the Burgundians in Hagen's telling (see note 981,4). Dietrich, however, is not impressed. See notes 1726,1; 2361,2.

1738,3 ■ See note 1657,3.

1739,3 ■ This is often taken to refer unmistakably to the Nibelung treasure, and hence to show either the old motif surviving incongruously, or Kriemhilde's mercenary mind, depending on whether a historical interpretation is the aim or not. It is worth recording, however, that this question of Kriemhilde's is a highly rhetorical one. She is reacting indignantly to Hagen's speech (1738), and demanding to know why he has the nerve to expect a welcome from her. We may assume, after all, that neither of them has forgotten about Sifrid's murder. Her question: "What have you brought me, that you should expect such a welcome?" refers unmistakably only to the total injury done her by Hagen. If he had brought back Sifrid from the dead, or the treasure from the Rhine, that might have been a sign of willingness to make amends. When pressed (1740), she refers specifically to the treasure (1741,2), perhaps as the only practical possibility. On hearing that the treasure too is irrevocably lost, she reverts to general terms (1743,2), and her second use of *mîn eigen* (1743,3) could equally well refer to Sifrid himself (see also note 821,3–4). Hagen's final answer (1744) is equally unspecific. By detailing his armour as the only gift he carries with him, he repudiates Kriemhilde's right to expect anything but enmity from him. His last brutal and provocative flaunting of Sifrid's sword is a fitting conclusion.
See also notes 1783 and 2372, where the sword and restitution

are still the theme, and sorrow for the treasure is completely merged in sorrow for Sifrid.[13]

1744,4 ▣ See also notes 1739,3; 1783; 2372.

1746,4 ▣ Looking after his own valuables is something of an obsession with Hagen. See also note 447,2 for the reluctance to give up his weapons, and note 531,2 for his use of the word *kameraere* in this connection.

1763–1764 ▣ Kriemhilde's technique here (especially 1763,1), as with Dietrich (1747; 1983), is substantially the same as Brünnhilde's (stanza 863). It is only that Hagen is now the object instead of the instrument, and with some justification. By acting for Brünnhilde, he accepted the compulsion of the "snarl and snivel" technique, and it is only fitting that it should now be turned against him. Perhaps this is why he is the only one to see the danger in Kriemhilde's invitation. The other Burgundians never pay more than lip-service to the more awkward demands of their women.

However different in their positive demands, Kriemhilde and Brünnhilde are very similar in their negative effects. Having lost what they wanted, they both use their residual position in society to force it into logical, consistent and inevitable self-destruction.

1771,3 ▣ Hagen's personal *übermuot* is an important contributory factor to the final disaster (as to Sifrid's murder): it makes Kriemhilde's task of stirring up ill feeling much easier (1898,4), alienates Etzel (who seeks to preserve the peace 1894,4) by the murder of his son, and rejects even Dietrich's final offer of safeconduct (stanza 2338). Had Hagen's character been more like

---

[13] Werner Schröder, "Die Tragödie Kriemhilts im *Nibelungenlied*," *Zeitschrift für deutsches Altertum*, Vol. XC (1960–61), p. 67, believes that the treasure gradually becomes for Kriemhilde a symbol of Sifrid. Perhaps it would be truer to say that both Sifrid and the treasure are symbols of her congenital inability to be contained by her environment. Schröder also remarks that this obsession of Kriemhilde's gives her a touch of humanity and greatness (pp. 154–5). The "humanity" fits into our analysis of Kriemhilde; the "greatness" does not, unless it is great to remain adolescent and demanding to one's last breath.

Dietrich's (who, for instance, is willing to forego blood vengeance, stanza 2336), the course of events would have been very different; compare, for example, the revealing stanza 1865, which suggests a limit to the "fatalism" of the work. See also notes 1783; 1792,4.

For a full and illuminating discussion of *übermuot* in the *Nibelungenlied*, see W. Hempel, "*Superbia als Schuldmotiv im Nibelungenlied*," *Seminar*, Vol. II (1966).

1779,2 ▪ It is only Volker's support which enables Hagen to go his own way, careless of what the three kings would prefer.

See also note 1476,1.

1781 ▪ The danger of being thought a coward drives Hagen to reject Kriemhilde's public, political status (cf. 1780,1–3). Much earlier, the Burgundians had used the same threat to force him to their way of thinking over Kriemhilde's invitation (1462,2). On that occasion, Hagen had been aware of her real motives (1461,4), while the Burgundians had concentrated on her official status as reconciled sister (1460,1–2). In both cases, the act which is called cowardly would have meant avoiding a personal clash between Hagen and Kriemhilde. The Burgundians had known this, but believed they at least could remain uninvolved (1460,4).

By now, Hagen has lost faith in any political solution to his feud with Kriemhilde. In neither case could the accusation of cowardice have stuck. Refusing Kriemhilde's invitation would have been politically wise, showing insight and caution rather than fear; admitting now her status as Queen of the Huns would be reasonable courtesy, and Volker, who is certainly not a coward, and not even particularly cautious, suggests it himself (stanza 1780).

In these contexts, bravery means something close to blindness, or refusing to consider the consequences; *vorhte*, on the other hand, as the narrator muses in stanza 1801, has its positive side.

1783 ▪ Yet another indication that Hagen has in some sense superseded Sifrid (see also notes 55,4; 1572,3–4; 1657,3). Hagen's action is provocative, like all his behaviour to Kriemhilde, and the provocation is remarkably successful. The sight of his suggestively flaunted sword has a profound effect on Kriemhilde, in striking contrast to Brünnhilde's indifference (see 447,2). This is natural enough, and puts Hagen and Kriemhilde together in a category which excludes Brünnhilde. (See also note 898,1–2.) Admittedly, much of the effect produced on Kriemhilde results from the sword's being Sifrid's, but it remains true that Hagen is the only man who has any right to wear it. It is fitting that of all the men she causes to be killed, only Hagen has the honour of being decapitated by her own fair hand. The whole pattern (clinging and quarrelling, leading to symbolic castration) is reminiscent of sibling rivalry.

See also note 1771,3.

1792,4 ◘ The irony is strong here, in the use of the stock adjective *übermüete*, so soon after its powerful occurrence in 1783,1. Compare 1821,4.

1807,3–4 ◘ *tugende pflegen*, a conventional phrase for excellence and correct behaviour, takes on a more practical flavour in the case of Wolfhart, who later loses his tenuous hold on propriety (2260 ff.).

1813–14 ◘ The contrast between this statement and the preceding scenes (cf. especially 1800,1–2) is blatant. For a cumulative and undifferentiated account of Etzel's unawareness, see Gottfried Weber, *Das Nibelungenlied: Problem und Idee* (Stuttgart, 1963), pp. 75–83.

1827,1 ◘ Compare 2001,1.
See also notes 1852–6; 1999–2002.

1828,3 ◘ See note 55,4.

1852–6 ◘ Hagen here explicitly refers to the contrast between earlier ceremonies and this one. Fine clothing is no longer needed. Mass is the prelude to death. In fact, the whole feast planned by Kriemhilde, the last of a long line of such celebrations, becomes a blood-bath, and all the virtues earlier extolled at such

length are now stripped of pretension. Hospitality (1828), jousting (1892), eating and drinking (2114), even the obligatory eagerness (*dringen*, 1866) to see the fair ladies (*schouwen*, 1869) now take on a menacing aspect. Innocent tedium gives way to imminent danger. None of these conventions seems to act positively any more.
See also note 1999–2002.

1856,1 ■ In one sense, this is a general exhortation to the Burgundians to remember their sins before dying, and as such it is hardly characteristic of Hagen. Perhaps, after dismissing the real chaplain (stanzas 1575–1580), he is forced to step into his shoes, as he did with Sifrid and the ferryman. On the other hand, that dismissal was most unceremonious, and closely related to Hagen's consciousness of solidarity among the Burgundians (1580,4), whatever the kings might still have hoped (1578,4; contrast 1576,3–4; 1577). On the whole, it must be admitted that Hagen's chaplaincy has a history and a flavour of its own, and one function of his exhortation is to produce a feeling of communal guilt in the Burgundians.

1859,4 ■ *dringen* almost certainly means here "meet, jostle, perhaps with dangerous consequences," but not specifically "attack" (e.g. 1867,4). In stanza 1803, it appears to mean "hem in, come too close for comfort." See also note 1852–6.

1865,4 ■ *ir* could mean either "her" (G. Weber, *Das Nibelungenlied* [1963], p. 107) or "their" (W. Schröder, "Die Tragödie Kriemhilts" [1960–61], p. 143). If Kriemhilde is meant, we learn nothing much from the line, since she has enough motives for concealing her hatred without adding *übermuot*. If the Burgundians are meant, we have an interesting side light on their behaviour. Not only Hagen's stubbornness and conscious defiance, but also the self-delusion of the kings (stanzas 1459–63) is classed as *übermuot*.
See also note 1131,3–4.

1874,3–4 ■ Dietrich's unique position makes one wonder if he could not have tried to warn Etzel, as well as save his own troops; but here as always he is content to do the least he can.

1887,1–3 ■ Gunther's laissez-faire attitude to the outbreak of war, like his continuing concern with appearances, does nothing to stave off the final disaster.

1891,1–2 ■ Hagen and Volker at last begin to attain one important goal: to make the three kings rally to their side, to heal the breach that has threatened to divide the Burgundians ever since Etzel wooed Kriemhilde, and to prevent the kings from entering too close an alliance with Etzel. The goal is finally attained in stanza 1968. By stanza 2089, a similar solidarity and intransigence has been established between Kriemhilde and Etzel.

1900–1 ■ The two versions of Kriemhilde's motives are here equated. The one rough and ready, desire for the treasure, the other more sophisticated, revenge for Sifrid. The same two levels of interpretation are enacted at the end, where Dietrich puts Hagen into the only hands that can, or have the right to, exact revenge for Sifrid (cf. 1901,3–4), and Hildebrant hastily disposes of a woman who can cause so much trouble.

Apart from the much discussed question of loyalty to Kriemhilde (hardly borne out by 1903,1), it is obvious that Dietrich has considerable understanding of and sympathy for her attitude.

1902,4 ■ See note 343,4.

1917,4 ■ Note the very restrained aside the narrator tucks in between Etzel's magnificent expression of unawareness and Hagen's dry retort.

1924,3 ■ Dankwart's lie is perhaps motivated by the hope of saving the men entrusted to his charge; when he finds this hope is vain, he regrets his plea for peace (1926,2).

1928,3–4 ■ The question of how Dankwart in particular came to know of Kriemhilde's particular bribe to Bloedelin is trivial in context. The overall pattern of Kriemhilde's behaviour is plain by now, and Dankwart's taunt to Bloedelin can stand for anyone who fondly hopes to gain from the catastrophe.

The triviality is nicely brought out in the phrase *ein vil getriuwer Hiune*. The Huns generally are not noted for anything but greed and fear in the *Nibelungenlied*; furthermore, if *getriuwe* means anything at all by this stage, it would have to mean "loyalty to Etzel, or to Kriemhilde." This obscure informant would have to be a very mixed-up Hun, and as such could also stand as one example of the total confusion and break-down of loyalties.

The narrator's embarrassment is similar to that which he shows in stanza 1477. Fortunately he does not always feel the need to draw our attention to such trivialities (see note 2229,4).

See also note 917,3-4.

1946,3-4 ▪ This closely echoes 916,3-4. In both cases, there is the same hunting image, the hunted animal stands for a man in danger of his life, and the narrator rhetorically points to the bravery involved. By momentarily equating the hunted Dankwart with the hunted Sifrid, the narrator also equates the present Huns with the earlier Burgundians. The bravery is now, with less irony, given to the hunted.

1960,3 ▪ One may doubt whether "drinking love" is an unambiguous reference to Germanic celebrations of the dead or to the practices of mediaeval guilds—though doubtless these extratextual associations made the use of the phrase in this context both possible to the poet and suggestive to some of his public. But to drink love and repay the king's wine by killing his son is a striking and effective image in itself, especially since wine functions in the poem as a measure of hospitality (e.g. 126,4; 804,2; 965 ff.; 1981,4; 2114). Hagen's ironic offer to make good the hospitality offered him comes with great effect after Dankwart has assumed the role of treasurer=murderer at the door (1958).

See also notes 804,2; 1852-6; 2114.

1960,4 ▪ There is something brutally ironic about giving the title *der junge vogt der hiunen* to this helpless infant just as it is to be killed. The effect comes partly from the formality of the term, and partly from the pretentious claims to power which it formalizes. As a function pure and simple (1135,2; 522,4), *voget* means something like "protector" or "authorized representative." As a respectful title, it is applied to Gunther nine times, Dietrich four times, Rüdeger three times, Liudeger twice, and Etzel once. Its use here is perhaps akin to some expression such as "his infant majesty."

1962,1 ■ It is true that this action would only appear just and reasonable in a version of the story where the child had disgraced the tutor (see de Boor, note to this line). But the point of Hagen's rage, and indeed the whole catastrophe, is precisely that it is not just, does not distinguish nicely between who merits death and who does not.

1968 ■ This is the first and almost last time that Gunther's alleged heroism is shown in action. It is also the point where he finally fails as king and peace-maker (1967,2; 1968, 1). The two things are brought together, as if they were two aspects of the same situation, as if heroism (or brute force) were nothing but the last resort when kingship (or civilization) breaks down. It was this ambivalence towards more primitive, less sophisticated behaviour patterns that drove the Burgundians first to harness Sifrid, and then to murder him.

Etzel is a more consistent king-figure than Gunther, in that he never shows any heroism at all (2020 ff.). Like Dietrich, however, he is unable to keep completely clear of the general degeneration, and loses all his men. The essentially social nature of the contract between king and subjects is pathetically spot-lighted when he is left to his own resources (1982,4).

See also note 2012,1.

1982,4 ■ See note 1968.

1983,3 ■ While kingship crumbles, Kriemhilde is quite clear about the demands she makes on law and order (cf. also 1985,2). Kings and virtues (*tugende*) are there to preserve her, whatever she is trying to do. In the present case, she must be preserved in order to destroy society. She chooses the only man who is still detached enough to help, but detachment has its disadvantages too (see note 1986).

1986 ■ Dietrich is the only character who actually seems to enjoy the carnage at this point. He is both detached and fascinated, and this ambivalent attitude is reflected in his ambiguous fate: he survives the slaughter, and yet loses all his men.

1994,4 ■ Gunther's attitude is very different from Hagen's (1967), and once again (see notes 872; 1204,3) he belatedly enforces his will (1990,3). But the result is an arbitrary compromise, not a just discrimination: Kriemhilde's son is slaughtered, while she herself escapes: Etzel is allowed out, but not his men (1999).

1999–2002 ■ So much for Etzel's protection, much vaunted as a great and extensive power for peace in the land (e.g. 1494).

The reason for his final humiliation comes in the second of these stanzas (2000,3), and is exactly the same as Gunther's, namely, the introduction of alien forces, or geste, as the Burgundians are repeatedly called (cf. 2002,4). The force of gast as applied to Sifrid at Worms (977,4) is now apparent, as also is Gunther's involuntary choice of a hospitality image when talking of his disastrous introduction of Brünnhilde (want ich hân den übeln tiuvel heim ze hûse geladen 649,2). Etzel's horror at the sight of Volker has much in common with Gunther's at the thought of his wife.

The horror is expressed (2001) in the form of an intolerable mixture of categories. The "feast" irony (cf. 1827,1 owê der nahtselde; 2122,4 ein arge hôhzît) is taken up in wê der hôhgezîte; the paradox of eber wilde—und ist ein spilman breaks down the comforting barriers between courtly functions; the final image of the devil driving the King out of his own hall recalls Gunther's description of Brünnhilde as the devil in his own home (649,2).

Volker is a good vehicle for Etzel's final realisation of his fatal mistake (2002,4), but, in fact, it would be his original importation of Kriemhilde which started everything. She is the real devil, or *leide gast*, although she never shows her hand clearly enough to make Etzel say so. Perhaps this is because she prefers (right up to her last murder, which brings swift punishment) to remain passive, to use the court in order to destroy it, whereas Brünnhilde's method was active rejection of the court's conventions.

See also notes 1763–64; 1852–6; 1983,3; 2114.

2005–7 ■ Apart from the necessity to ride this rather flat image (bow=sword) to death, Hagen's speech seems permeated with a heavy, if obscure irony. There is the rather obvious point that neither Volker nor Hagen will live to see any of these rewards. Could Hagen also be mocking at the judge-and-rewarder function that Gunther has at last thrown away by joining the fight (1968)?

At all events, and whatever Hagen's intention, the speech helps to emphasize the enormity of the present break-down, by still assuming a continuity that everyone knows has been disrupted. Volker's deserts (promotion, 2005; reasonable reward, 2007,4) are expressed in the most peace-time and prosaic way.

2012,1 ■ Hagen may well be pleased: at last the kings are seeing things his way; that is, they have ceased to be kings and have become fighting-men (see also 2104–6 and note 1968). Hagen exults in his achievement (2020), and nearly succeeds in dragging Etzel down to the same level (2022), but Etzel still has something to live for. He is not yet desperate enough for heroics.

See also note 2020–23.

2020–23 ■ Etzel appears ridiculous here, in that his own subjects have to restrain him (2022,3) from possibly disastrous valour. But his lack of heroism is only ridiculous according to the standards Hagen is trying to set up. Like Arthur in the Court Epic, Gunther before stanza 1968 and Dietrich throughout the *Nibelungenlied*, Etzel's function is that of detached judge and arbiter. Hagen has dragged down Gunther and the other kings (notes 1968; 2012,1), but does not succeed with Etzel.

Hagen's sneer in 2023,3 is justified only in the area of absolute power and absolute virility. This is, of course, the area where Etzel is no match for Sifrid (see note 1368). It is revealing that

Hagen's taunt is a clear echo of Kriemhilde's revelation to Brünnhilde (840,3), to the publication of which he objected so violently (867,3–4). He evidently has more respect for a king who conceals his inadequacies than for one who openly accepts a second-hand wife.

The attitude of Hagen and Kriemhilde to the possible threat of Sifrid's pre-eminence is typically Burgundian. They both use it to undermine others, but cannot see how it undermines their own position. For both of them, Sifrid's possession of Brünnhilde and Kriemhilde is, in the end, fatal. For Etzel it is not (however ignominious his survival).

Sifrid himself, on the other hand, has little interest in public status. He denies ever having boasted openly of his conquest of Brünnhilde (858), and seems to consider such a disclosure foolish and pointless (862), rather than politically disruptive. It is unthinkable that Sifrid himself would ever have used such a sneer as this one to Etzel.

The archaic ending of *vorderôst* (2020,2) emphasises the sneer. Compare 1526,1, where it seems fairly harmless, and 1012,3 note.

2060,4 ■ Iring's first scuffle with the Burgundians has a touch of burlesque—perhaps because they think he is hardly worth bothering about (stanza 2029). But when he attacks them a second time, Hagen feels it is too much and shows him no mercy. The comic regrets his rashness too late (2068).

It is clear from the whole work that heroism in the style of Hagen is less a positive value than a last desperate reaction to imminent and unavoidable danger (see also note 2012,1). The comedy of the present scene is functional, in that these particular heroics are not even necessary. Iring's attempt to chase personal honour (2036,3), when everyone else fights reluctantly and out of necessity, has something in common with Volker's exaggerated prowess. But Volker's exuberance is subservient to Hagen's sense of necessity.

2087,4 ▣ Hagen and Volker take no part in this late attempt of the three kings to make peace. It has no chance of success, since they have forfeited their right to this sort of activity (see note

2012,1), and now that he has lost his son and many of his men, Etzel's desire for revenge is nearly as great as his wife's—and she will only make peace if the kings hand over Hagen, which they in turn refuse to do (2105–7). The ranks are quite closed now on both sides, even the link between Kriemhilde and Giselher (note 1078,3) is finally severed (2103,1).

The actual details of the parley provide an uncomfortably modern picture of injured innocence and righteous indignation on both sides.

2100 ◼ Kriemhilde's persistent identification with the Burgundians comes out here. She is still proud of their prowess, disdainful of the Huns, and still looking for a chance to confront her own family face to face.

2104,1–2 ◼ That Kriemhilde waits till it is too late before offering to accept Hagen as scapegoat may testify to her inner urge to destroy the whole society in which she was brought up (rather than "purify" it, cf. note 1031). But the offer also raises the question: would the Burgundian kings at any stage have been willing to sacrifice Hagen? Certainly their tender consciences and lack of moral fibre would have made them receptive to the *idea* (cf. note 1204,3). But to act upon it, and to survive afterwards, they would presumably have needed someone else to depend on in his place. The only possible candidate is Kriemhilde herself: which perhaps helps explain why Hagen had to harass her—before she could effectively work upon them and harass him (cf. note 1136,4). See also note 1256,2.

2114 ◼ See note 804,2

H. B. Willson, "Blood and Wounds in the *Nibelungenlied*," *Modern Language Review*, Vol. LV (1960), pp. 42–3, is very conscious of the Christian symbolism of this blood-drinking. He takes 2114,3 seriously, and interprets stanza 2115 as an act of religious importance, followed by the gift of renewed strength. We feel that such an interpretation ignores the implied contrast with earlier, less gruesome feasts, and the fact that this is real human blood, and real carnage. See also note 1999–2002.

2120–3 ▣ The exhaustion of the Burgundians seems to be reflected in the repetitious feebleness of their observations.

2122,4 ▣ See notes 1503,2–4; 1999–2002.

2142 ▣ This uncharacteristic behaviour of Rüdeger shows something of the extremity of his frustration. He is faced with an intolerable decision, unable to act without betraying his deepest convictions (stanza 2154). Eventually he chooses one course, not because it is preferable, but because it promises the final irresponsibility of death (2163,4; 2164). At the moment he has not yet given up, and his murder of the Hun is a neat displacement pattern. The provocation (2141,3) and the response are more in Hagen's style than Rüdeger's (1464; 1560–62), but it is a good example to follow just before he finally settles down to characteristic and fussy impotence.

Gottfried Weber, *Das Nibelungenlied: Problem und Idee* (Stuttgart, 1963), pp. 91 ff., sees Rüdeger's choice as a rejection of Christian chivalry in favour of "Heldentum," symbolized by his emphasis on personal *êre* (2154,3; 2156,4; 2218,3). But while there is no doubt that Rüdeger does lose hold of the image he has lived by, it is also true that this defeat is forced on him precisely by this image (see notes 2166,3–4; 2196–2197). Heroism and honour in battle are not an alternative to his earlier commitment, but rather the inevitable result of carrying his values to extremes. As always in the *Nibelungenlied*, individual heroism is negatively presented. It is the only thing left when socially more developed behaviour-patterns break down.

2148,1 ▣ The unity of purpose between herself and Etzel which Kriemhilde has managed to bring about is vital to her success when she comes to put pressure on Rüdeger, even if it makes something less than a majestic emperor out of Etzel.
See note 2152, 1–2.

2150,3 ▣ *sêle* here is not specifically the Christian soul, but whatever gives value to life in this world: for Rüdeger, the fulfilment of his obligations to his friends (cf. 2156 and note 1656 ff.). In his present dilemma Rüdeger can be confident of proving his honour (êre) as a fighting-man, but he can find no way out of a moral dilemma which threatens the very core of his being (sêle).

In this sense many people have a sêle: some simple code by which their moral selves live (such as "doing what is right"). In Western civilization the problems of conscience which are liable to result from such a code have been much investigated by saints and writers—which may explain why scholars often react to Rüdeger as "Christian" or "modern."

Rüdeger's invocation of his Creator (2154,4) is of course no more than a pious hope that higher authority will solve his problem for him, similar to his vain plea to Etzel (2157). Bert Nagel's attempt (Das Nibelungenlied: Stoff, Form, Ethos [Frankfurt-am-Main; 1965], pp. 205–65) to give importance to the Christian elements occurring here and elsewhere in the poem seems to us as mistaken as his championship of Rüdeger's character.

2152,1–2 ■ The phrase sich ze füezen bieten, in the sense of "prostrate oneself to extract a favour," is used also when Iring begs his relatives to let him return to fight Hagen. (Its only other occurrence in the work describes the due homage paid to their new master Gunther by Brünnhilde's men). De Boor (note to this line) points out this parallel between Etzel and Iring, and raises the question of whether the phrase is to be taken literally or not. He decides: yes for Etzel and Kriemhilde; no for Iring. Admittedly, Iring is not a very serious character, and does not last long. But Etzel has also lost dignity since stanza 2001. Bracketing them together reinforces the common impression of exaggerated behaviour. Iring is over-eager to get killed. Etzel goes farther than regal dignity requires, and perhaps it is his desire to please Kriemhilde that leads him to join her in her characteristic posture and favourite role of poor, defenceless woman. She certainly takes over the conduct of the scene in stanza 2147, and presumes to speak for Etzel (2148,1).[14]

---

[14] P. Wapnewski, "Rüdigers Schild. Zur 37. Aventiure des Nibelungenliedes," Euphorion LIV (1960), p. 390, points out that this gesture also has the legal significance of a plea for mercy, which would add to the enormity of Kriemhilde's behaviour when she uses it as an incitement to more killing.

2163,2 ▣ See note 343,4. The self-reference implies here both self-pity and detachment.

2166,3–4 ▣ It is nowhere suggested in the text that the priority Rüdeger gives to the claims of Etzel and Kriemhilde to his allegiance is rational, or based on chronology, as has been argued. His dilemma is insoluble: whatever he does, he must fail in one obligation or another. What he proceeds to do is to choose the course which leads to his death. It is a personal choice, determined by his particular character. He could equally well have elected to fail Etzel and Kriemhilde—and go into exile. But to stand outside the supports of society in this way, he would have to be a Dietrich, not a Rüdeger. It is significant that Rüdeger early on (1681,4–1682,1) sees himself as essentially dependent on Etzel, and gives this as a reason for his great reliance on loyalty (triuwen 1682,1) and generosity (1682,2) as substitutes for independent wealth and power (1681,4). Dietrich is the only man who twice survives complete independence. None of the others ever conceives of this way out. Rüdeger can only envisage it as something the king might do for him (stanza 2157). When the king refuses, that way is blocked.[15]
See also note 2142.

2171 ▣ It may be true that Giselher's youth has something to do with his optimism here (see de Boor, note to 2170,4), but he is not noticeably different from the other Burgundians in this (see note 1078,3). Compare Gunther's confidence 2177,4 and Gernot's, stanza 2182. Indeed, the contrast between Giselher's blindness and Volker's realism is reminiscent of the undifferentiated Burgundian reaction to Hagen's early warnings (e.g. Gunther, stanza 1460; Gernot, 1462; Giselher, 1463). The Burgundians, apart from Hagen and Volker, appear to have learnt very little.

2188,1 ▣ There is a certain tension as to whether Gernot is still

---

[15] P. Wapnewski, "Rüdigers Schild," p. 393, sees Rüdeger's decision as forced on him by Germanic law. Legally, he was not bound to the Burgundians at all. But it would be misleading to emphasize this (however many "termini technici" [p. 382] the scene may contain), when the whole pattern of Rüdeger's behaviour has led so clearly to his present dilemma, which is quite a real one.

speaking, which is only resolved at 2189,4. Thus the poet emphasizes that Rüdeger must fight not only Gernot, who carries his
sword, but also Giselher, who is betrothed to his daughter (see also
note 126,1). Only Hagen (and Volker), in a sense the man most
responsible for and least personally involved in the situation, finds
a way out of the dilemma (2201).

The momentary fusion of Gernot and Giselher into a sort of
composite son-figure is helped by Rüdeger's distribution of gifts
between them. Giselher gets his daughter, and becomes his son-
in-law; Gernot gets his sword, and becomes symbolically his heir
and superseder. This is why he can happily commend his wife
and daughter to Gernot, only to be answered by Giselher. The
genetic explanation usually offered (cf. de Boor, note) should not
be allowed to obscure what is happening. Rüdeger has identified
himself with the conventions that hold people together in society.
When the society breaks up he is torn apart.

2196–97 ■ Attention has traditionally been concentrated on
whether this generous gesture is essentially "heroic" or "chivalrous" or both.[16]

A more accessible problem is the effect that it produces here.
It is the last of a long series of gifts, material and spiritual, given
by Rüdeger, with the original intention of cementing relationships together (see also notes 1634; 2188,1). The others—a sword
to Gernot, his daughter to Giselher, hospitality to the Burgundians, protection to Kriemhilde, loyalty to Etzel—all combine to
break him.

The situation is slightly different with this gift of a shield to
Hagen. In the first place, the original gift at Bechelaren was not
Rüdeger's idea, and formed no part of his or his wife's plans. In
fact, it was not so much given, as demanded by Hagen; something
much treasured and reluctantly surrendered (stanza 1698).

---

[16] Cf. de Boor, note to 2196,2.
  In particular, both P. Wapnewski, "Rüdigers Schild. Zur 37. Aventiure des
Nibelungenliedes," *Euphorion* LIV (1960), and Gottfried Weber, *Das Nibelungenlied: Problem und Idee* (Stuttgart, 1963), take this very seriously. See
pp. 200 ff. in Weber's book for a summary of the discussion. See also note
2142 of this Commentary.

Furthermore, it turns out to be of limited use, and has to be replaced; more willingly this time, but still presumably for a limited
period only. There seems to be something pathetically inadequate
about everything Rüdeger has to offer. It is as if he tries to cover
up the primitive basis of relationships by typing people around
him as recognizably innocuous members of society. The checks
and balances are lost once Etzel's authority breaks down, and
Gernot-Giselher, the composite son-in-law (see note 2188,1), becomes a primitive danger instead; the inheritor of his sword is not
necessarily his friend for life. With Hagen he does manage to
make a private agreement, a sort of two-man society, but their
truce has no effect on their eventual fate.

2213,1 ■ See note 1960,4.

2229,4 ■ The unconcern shown in the poem for the logic of
everyday life is well exemplified here, where Volker "answers"
a speech one would not expect him to have heard. (Compare the
"Wechsel" technique in Minnesang.)
    See also note 1928,3–4.

2230,2 ■ The vicious mockery of this pseudo-courtesy goes well
with the adjective *zierlîch* (2229,4).
    P. Wapnewski, "Rüdigers Schild" (1960), p. 397, sees Volker's
speech here as a sign that the Burgundians were "Wissende und
Verzeihende," especially when Volker pays his tribute to the
dead Rüdeger in 2231,4. This approach ignores the self-inflicted
nature of Rüdeger's dilemma, and also the bitterness in Volker's
tribute. Rüdeger certainly has "served Kriemhilde to the end,"
but what good has it done anyone?

2238,2 ■ Dietrich is just counselling caution and understanding
for the other person's point of view: a quality very rare in the
work, but decisive for him (stanza 2336). Unlike Rüdeger, he
appears to owe no specific allegiance to Etzel, but he does later
admit a moral obligation to Rüdeger (stanza 2317).

2246,4 ■ There is no need to import any past incidents to justify
this remark. Its function is clear enough, in that it refers once

more to Rüdeger's characteristic helpfulness: the quality that caught him up in the fighting, and which now apparently can still work after his death to involve Dietrich's men.

See notes 2188,1; 2196–97.

2249,4 ▪ It is revealing for the general import of the *Nibelungenlied* that this fallacy, for many years now one of the main buttresses of "the conventional wisdom," is relegated to an obviously inadequate character like Wolfhart. In the event, he himself ensures that no other potentialities of human behaviour will find expression. The reductive power of a limited intelligence is nicely illustrated (and tersely formulated in 2250,1), and only Dietrich and Hildebrand are left alive.

That Dietrich does not exert enough control over his lieutenants to ensure that they carry out his wishes is of course one reason why he ends up on his own. Observant and reflective, he is too detached and resigned to force his will upon others.

2265–66 ▪ Once more the possibility of reconciliation, kept open by Hildebrand and Gunther, is closed, this time by Volker and Wolfhart—with what consequences one only realizes when one remembers that so far, of the Burgundian leaders, only Gernot has fallen. Later, but only after the death of nearly all the rest, Gunther identifies himself with Volker's position (2335).

2279,2 ▪ Gunther's development from weak courtesy to fighting heroism makes this courtly formula particularly appropriate, especially since the downfall of civilized kingship was associated, for Etzel as well as Gunther, with the "reception" of unfortunately chosen "guests."

See also notes 977,4; 1999–2002.

2312,4 ▪ The line is nicely ambiguous: "If I intended to preserve my honour, I should have to kill you," or "If it wasn't a shameful thing to do, I'd kill you." Either way, Dietrich stands well outside the code of crime and punishment he is invoking. He has no intention whatever of killing Hildebrand, who is, after all, merely the side of Dietrich that can still get involved with other human beings.

See also note 2345,2.

2322,4 ▪ Dietrich's private hopes have been destroyed by a feud which did not concern him and which he did his utmost to keep out of. But the destruction of his hopes is necessary if he is to be preserved, together with Hildebrand, as a symbol of detachment, a man who survives the destruction of the society he is in, because his interest is always elsewhere.

B. Nagel, "Das Dietrichbild des Nibelungenliedes," *Zeitschrift für deutsche Philologie*, Vol. LXXVIII (1959), p. 268, sees Dietrich's self-preservation in a much nobler, more grandiose light: his emotional outbursts of sorrow and anger are interpreted as increasing the stature of his achievement in controlling them. The fact remains that his self-control achieves nothing for himself, or for the Burgundians. Both his neutrality and his final intervention are wasted.

2335–2338 ▪ Gunther has still not completely lost his touch, and the actual event referred to (vacillation on his part, emotional action on the part of others, 2264 ff.) is once more clothed in a rational and kingly garb.

His next decision (2338) is taken for him as rudely as ever by Hagen, who does not even let him speak. From the haste with which Hagen jumps in, he seems to fear that Gunther may be as civilized as ever (see also note 1968), and in danger of responding to Dietrich's invitation to act as he used to at Worms (*durch die zühte dîn*, 2336,2). Dietrich himself goes out of his way to address Gunther, evidently aiming at the weak spot, and treats Hagen as an appendage, which of course he is, according to the pretensions of the court at Worms. The contrast between 2337 (2nd person singular addressed to Gunther; Hagen an appendage with no say), and 2338 (Hagen answers roughly and Gunther never speaks) is quite startling at this late stage.

2345,2 ▪ In saying this Dietrich contemptuously dismisses a central feature of the heroic code: the "Trutzrede," with which opponents incite one another to battle.

In much the same way he dismisses Hagen's murder of Sifrid as not worth discussing (note 1726,1).

See also notes 2312,4; 2322,4.

2349 ▪ This is the only hint in the *Nibelungenlied* that a knight could use his intelligence while fighting.

2353,1–3 ▪ As Dietrich owes no specific obligation to Etzel or to Kriemhilde, presumably in handing Hagen and Gunther over to Kriemhilde (not Etzel!), he is simply acknowledging her claims as their chief enemy. Since they have refused to make a separate peace with him—which would apparently have abrogated these claims—he is content, when he has defeated them, to leave them to her mercy. In doing so, he relies on formulae (see note 2354–6), and shows little interest in the possible emotions underlying Kriemhilde's attitude to her captives. His indifference apparently extends to their final death at her hands. Hildebrand, on the other hand, who was involved (even wounded) in the disintegration, has to strike out at the cause of his involvement (note 2312,4).

Kriemhilde evidently means nothing whatever to Dietrich (see note 2354–2356). It is true that he weeps together with Etzel after Kriemhilde's death (2377,3), but there is no reason to suppose he is weeping specifically for her. The only information offered by the narrator (2377,4) would suggest that his grief is still directed towards his own loss (cf. stanzas 2319–2323).

See also note 500,1–3.

2354–2356 ▪ In using this formula *wie wol er iuch ergetzet* 2355,3), Dietrich formalizes a real issue, but at a most inappropriate moment. Restitution for the loss of Sifrid is indeed what Kriemhilde has wanted all along. On the other hand, it is unthinkable that Dietrich could still believe restitution possible in any normal sense (any more than he could take seriously Kriemhilde's protestation of lifelong devotion, 2354,4). He is, of course, taking up her own exclamation (2354,3), and using the same term *ergetzen*, but he suggests Hagen rather than himself as the pos-

sible benefactor. Is he just rejecting Kriemhilde's offer of grati-
tude? Or is he merely pandering to her paranoia? or could he be
honestly suggesting that Hagen (locked up and invisible, 2356,2)
would make a good *substitute* for Sifrid?

2361,2 ▪ The line emphasizes the ignobility of the way Gunther
and Hagen are in the end simply tied up by Dietrich and led
away (2362,1–2). The scene is reminiscent of an earlier occasion
(1995,1), when Dietrich had tucked Etzel under one arm, and
Kriemhilde under the other, and so saved them from certain death.
The parallel does not detract from the shame of Gunther's and
Hagen's defeat; nor does the ambiguous stature of Dietrich, who
appears great enough, but not so great that defeat at his hands is
necessarily glorious.[17] This then is what all the heroic defiance of
the two survivors has come to: being tied up like old sacks and
executed by a woman.

2361,3–4 ▪ According to these lines Dietrich's actions have some
positive motivation: to save such remnants of society as still
survive for the future.

2372 ▪ In this pathetic speech Kriemhilde returns to her hope of
restitution (*geltes*), which she now finally abandons. All she has
left is Sifrid's sword, and a naïve, almost girlish memory of Sifrid
still fresh in her mind (*mîn holder vriedel*). In this mood of utter
defeat, and realizing at last that her loss is final and irrevocable,
she takes revenge on Hagen. There is nothing else she can do, and
the negative nature of her action is emphasized by her own immediate despatch. There is of course a grandeur in avenging her
husband's murder with her murdered husband's sword. But it is
the grandeur of a primitive society. For the Burgundians, includ-

---

[17] J. K. Bostock, "The Message of the *Nibelungenlied*," *Modern Language
Review*, Vol. LV (1960), p. 212, believes that all the characters in the book
except Dietrich are guilty of the sin of pride. This final humiliation is thus a
fitting punishment. (He also believes that Dietrich symbolizes "God the Judge",
although God does not characteristically lose all his men and weep). See
the analysis by W. Hempel of the *Nibelungenlied* in terms of *superbia*, in
great detail and some over-emphasis, "Superbia als Schuldmotiv im *Nibelungenlied*," *Seminar*, Vol. II (1966).

ing Kriemhilde, it is the last stage of their reduction and eventual
annihilation (cf. 2378,1).
  See also note 1739,3.

2376,4 ■ No more than Gunther and Hagen does Kriemhilde
come to a heroic end : she is merely executed by Dietrich's lieuten-
ant, as one who has no further right to live (see also note
2353,1–3). The grandiose passion for restitution which has gradually ousted all other emotions in her, like the heroic defiance to
which Gunther rises (or is reduced), have both contributed their
share to the story; but the sum total, the final issue to which
everything leads, is not glory, but annihilation (2378–9). Only
non-participants survive.

2377,2 ■ This line is a terse summing up of the disintegration of
formal society, demonstrated in the career of one member. From
edel to *ze stücken*; from close-knit nobility, with all its exemplary
tedium, to heroic fragments.